1300 CA

MEAL PLAN FOR

WEIGHT LOSS

The Comprehensive Guide to Healthy and Delicious low carb and high protein recipes to lose weight and Live Longer.

David T. Salcedo

COPYRIGHT

All rights reserved. No part of this publication may be reproduced, distributed, or transmitted in any form or by any means, including photocopying, recording, or other electronic or mechanical methods, without the prior written permission of the publisher, except in the case of brief quotations embodied in critical reviews and certain other noncommercial uses permitted by copyright law.

Copyright © 2024 by David T. Salcedo

HOW TO MAKE USE OF THIS COOKBOOK

Get acquainted with the cookbook

Begin by reading the introduction and any directions included with the cookbook. Understand the 1300-calorie meal plan's ideas as well as the underlying thought behind the meals.

Calculate Your Caloric Needs

Determine whether a 1300-calorie plan is appropriate for your weight loss goals. Consider talking with a healthcare expert or nutritionist to ensure that the strategy meets your specific requirements.

Evaluate your current eating habits

Evaluate your existing eating habits and preferences. Determine where alterations can be made to comply with the 1300-calorie meal plan. This could include reducing portion sizes, using healthier products, or adjusting cooking methods.

Plan Your Meals

Create a weekly meal plan based on the cookbook's recipes. Ensure that your meals are nutritionally balanced and varied. Consider taste preferences, dietary constraints, and convenience.

Create a Shopping List

Create a shopping list based on the ingredients needed for the selected recipes. This makes grocery shopping easier and ensures you have everything you need to stick to the meal plan.

Prepare Meals in Advance

Preparing meals ahead of time can help you stick to the 1300-calorie regimen. Batch cooking on weekends or evenings can save time during the week while reducing the temptation to choose less healthful options.

Portion Control

Pay attention to portion sizes to ensure you stay inside the 1300-calorie limit. Use measurement instruments or visual cues to ensure appropriate portion sizes, encouraging successful calorie management.

Stay Hydrated

Make it a habit to drink the required amount of water each day. Hydration is an essential component of any weight loss program and adds to overall health.

Monitor Progress

Regularly evaluate your progress. Keep a meal log, monitor weight changes, or take note of energy increases. Adjust your meal plan as needed based on your personal response.

Seek Support and Maintain Consistency

Weight loss journeys can be hard. Seek assistance from friends, family, and online networks. Consistency is essential, so stick to the 1300-calorie meal plan, make necessary tweaks, and celebrate your accomplishments along the way.

TABLE OF CONTENTS

How to Make Use of this Cookbook 3
INTRODUCTION 13
What is 1300 Calorie Diet................................. 16
Overview of the 1300 Calorie Diet 17
Who Can Benefit from a 1300 Calorie Diet 20
Understanding Calories.................................... 23
    How Many Calories Do You Need.................. 24
Choosing the Right Proteins, Carbs, and Fats...... 25
    Proteins.. 25
    Carbohydrates... 25
    Fats 25
Hydration Role in 1300 Calorie Diet Meal Plan..... 27
    Creating Hydration Ideas 28
Meal Planning 30
Overcoming Challenges During 1300 Calorie Diet Plan.. 32
    Addressing Hunger and Cravings 32
        Strategies for Managing Hunger.............. 32
Addressing cravings....................................... 33
Social and lifestyle challenges 33
Staying Motivated on a 1300 Calorie Diet 35
Common Mistake to Avoid 37
CHAPTER 1 40

Breakfast Recipes 40
1. Greek Yogurt Parfait with Berries and Almonds ... 40
2. Vegetable Omelette with Whole Wheat Toast 42
3. Overnight Chia Seed Pudding 44
4. Avocado and Egg Toast............ 45
5. Berry and Spinach Smoothie Bowl 47
6. Whole Grain Pancakes with Mixed Berries 49
7. Spinach and Feta Breakfast Wrap............ 51
8. Protein-Packed Berry Smoothie 53
9. Egg White and Vegetable Scramble 54
10. Cottage Cheese and Pineapple Bowl 56
11. Oatmeal with Banana and Almond Butter.......... 57
12. Smoked Salmon and Cream Cheese Bagel.......... 59
13. Peanut Butter and Banana Smoothie 60
14. Vegetarian Breakfast Burrito 62
15. Cinnamon Apple Quinoa Bowl............ 64
16. Chia Seed and Berry Smoothie............ 65
17. Turkey and Vegetable Breakfast Wrap 67
18. Cottage Cheese Pancakes 69
19. Mushroom and Spinach Scramble 70
20. Blueberry Almond Overnight Oats............ 72

CHAPTER 2 74
Lunch Recipes 74

1. Quinoa and Vegetable Power Bow 74
2. Turkey and Veggie Stir-Fry 76
3. Salmon and Quinoa Stuffed Bell Peppers 78
4. Mediterranean Chickpea Wrap 81
5. Tofu and Vegetable Stir-Fry with Brown Rice 83
6. Chickpea and Spinach Salad with Lemon-Tahini Dressing 85
7. Shrimp and Avocado Wrap 87
8. Egg and Vegetable Stir-Fry with Quinoa 89
9. Black Bean and Vegetable Burrito Bowl 91
10. Caprese Salad with Grilled Chicken 93
11. Mango and Shrimp Quinoa Salad 95
12. Chicken and Vegetable Brown Rice Bowl 97
13. Spinach and Feta Stuffed Chicken Breast 99
14. Vegetarian Lentil and Sweet Potato Chili 101
15. Turkey and Quinoa Stuffed Bell Peppers 103
16. Vegetarian Quinoa and Black Bean Bow 105
17. Asian-Inspired Tofu and Vegetable Stir-Fry 107
18. Mediterranean Quinoa Salad with Chickpeas 110
19. Salmon and Asparagus Foil Pack 113
20. Caprese Wrap with Turkey 115

CHAPTER 3 117
Dinner Recipes 117
1. Grilled Salmon with Asparagus 117

2. Veggie and Chicken Skewers................................119
3. Quinoa and Chickpea Buddha Bowl................... 121
4. Turkey and Vegetable Stir-Fry............................. 122
5. Lentil and Vegetable Soup................................... 124
6. Eggplant and Chickpea Curry.............................. 126
7. Zucchini Noodles with Pesto and Cherry Tomatoes 129
8. Baked Sweet Potato and Black Bean Quesadillas 131
9. Spinach and Mushroom Stuffed Chicken Breast. 133
10. Broccoli and Tofu Stir-Fry................................. 135
11. Cauliflower Fried Rice with Shrimp.................. 137
12. Stuffed Bell Peppers with Turkey and Quinoa .. 139
13. Mediterranean Chickpea Salad.......................... 141
14. Spaghetti Squash with Turkey Bolognese 143
15. Grilled Veggie and Hummus Wrap.................... 145
16. Baked Chicken with Lemon and Rosemary 147
17. Chickpea and Spinach Stuffed Sweet Potatoes . 148
18. Teriyaki Salmon with Broccoli and Quinoa 151
19. Blackened Shrimp Tacos with Avocado Lime Crema.. 153
20. Quinoa and Black Bean Stuffed Bell Peppers... 155

CHAPTER 4 157
Side dishes recipes 157
1. Roasted Brussels Sprouts with Balsamic Glaze .. 157

2. Quinoa and Vegetable Stir-Fry 159
3. Cucumber and Tomato Salad with Feta 161
4. Sauteed Garlic Spinach 163
5. Baked Sweet Potato Wedges 165
6. Greek Salad with Chickpeas 167
7. Cauliflower Rice Pilaf 169
8. Steamed Asparagus with Lemon Garlic Sauce 171
9. Mushroom and Spinach Quiche Cups 173
10. Spaghetti Squash Primavera 175
11. Baked Zucchini Fries 177
12. Cabbage and Carrot Slaw 179
13. Eggplant and Tomato Bake 181
14. Mango Avocado Salsa 183
15. Cucumber Avocado Gazpacho 185
16. Brussels Sprouts and Apple Salad 187
17. Quinoa Stuffed Bell Peppers 189
18. Mediterranean Quinoa Salad 192

CHAPTER 5 194

Snacks Recipes 194
1. Greek Yogurt Parfait with Berries 194
2. Almond Butter and Banana Rice Cakes 195
3. Veggie Sticks with Hummus 197
4. Cottage Cheese and Pineapple Cups 198

5. Whole Grain Crackers with Avocado 199
6. Berry and Nut Smoothie Bowl 201
7. Roasted Chickpeas Snack 202
8. Cucumber Avocado Salsa 204
9. Edamame and Sea Salt Snack 206
10. Dark Chocolate and Almond Trail Mix 207
11. Crispy Kale Chips 209
12. Spiced Roasted Chickpea and Nut Mix 211
13. Caprese Skewers with Balsamic Glaze 213
14. Sweet Potato and Black Bean Salsa 214
15. Cinnamon Apple Chips 216
16. Avocado and Tomato Bruschetta 218

CHAPTER 6 220
  Desserts and treats 220
    1. Chia Seed Pudding with Mixed Berries 220
    2. Greek Yogurt Parfait with Nuts and Honey 222
    3. Baked Apples with Cinnamon and Oats 223
    4. Dark Chocolate and Berry Smoothie Bowl 225
    5. Frozen Banana and Peanut Butter Bites 227
    6. Coconut and Mango Chia Seed Popsicles 229
    7. Protein-Packed Chocolate Avocado Mousse 230
    8. Blueberry and Almond Yogurt Bark 232
    9. Peach and Raspberry Sorbet 233

10. Cinnamon Baked Pears with Yogurt 235
11. Strawberry and Basil Infused Watermelon Salad 236
12. Pineapple and Mint Sorbet 238
13. Chocolate-Dipped Strawberries with Almonds . 239
14. Avocado and Lime Frozen Yogurt 241
15. Cucumber and Mint Granita 242
16. Mango and Coconut Chia Seed Pudding 244
17. Cinnamon Roasted Plums with Greek Yogurt ... 245

CHAPTER 7 249

Beverages 249

1. Green Smoothie 249
2. Berry Yogurt Parfait 251
3. Iced Green Tea with Mint 252
4. Chia Seed Pudding 254
5. Chocolate Avocado Mousse 255
6. Fruit Infused Water 257
7. Frozen Banana Bites 259
8. Cucumber Mint Sorbet 260
9. Avocado and Berry Smoothie Bowl 262
10. Almond Butter and Banana Smoothie 264
11. Mango Coconut Chia Pudding 266
12. Blueberry and Almond Overnight Oats 268
13. Apple Cinnamon Protein Smoothie 270

14. Sweet Potato and Cinnamon Smoothie 271
15. Spinach and Pineapple Smoothie 273
16. Mediterranean Hummus Platter......................... 275
17. Greek Yogurt and Berry Parfait 276
18. Caprese Salad Skewers.. 278
19. Quinoa Salad with Roasted Vegetables 280
CHAPTER 8 282
  Conclusion.. 282

INTRODUCTION

Sarah, a young professional, comes to a crossroads when she realizes her sedentary lifestyle and improper eating habits are affecting her health. Motivated to reclaim control of her health, she chooses a 1300-calorie meal plan as the beginning point for her transforming journey.

The Decision to Change Sarah delves into the world of nutrition, attempting to understand the importance of calorie intake, portion control, and nutritional density. Recognizing the need for long-term adjustments, she decides to take a balanced approach that emphasizes both quality and quantity.

Sarah learns how to plan meals that balance proteins, carbohydrates, and fats while staying under a 1300-calorie restriction. The chapter digs into the creative process of meal planning, showcasing delectable meals that not only satisfy her palate but also provide her body with critical nutrients.

As Sarah explores the world of food, she learns the art of sensible nibbling. She learns to reduce cravings without sacrificing her daily calorie budget by practicing portion control and making smart food choices. The chapter outlines ways for avoiding typical snacking problems and maintaining discipline.

Sarah investigates several ways to incorporate water and other low-calorie beverages into her daily routine. The chapter emphasizes the importance of adequate hydration in helping her achieve her weight loss objectives and overall well-being.

To supplement her food modifications, Sarah incorporates a moderate but consistent exercise plan into her everyday life. The chapter delves into various forms of workouts appropriate for beginners, emphasizing the importance of combining physical activity with a 1300-calorie meal plan to achieve the best outcomes.

Sarah confronts a variety of challenges, ranging from occasional hunger sensations to social and lifestyle issues.

As Sarah improves, she acknowledges tiny successes and milestones along the road.

Sarah approaches her goal weight, the emphasis shifts to living a healthy and balanced lifestyle. The chapter delves into ways for moving from a regulated 1300-calorie meal plan to a sustainable, lifelong approach to nutrition and well-being.

Sarah discusses how the 1300-calorie meal plan evolved into a useful strategy for weight management rather than just weight loss. The chapter delves into how she adapted the diet to handle fluctuations, maintained a healthy connection with food, and found delight in nourishing her body.

WHAT IS 1300 CALORIE DIET

A 1300 calorie diet is a calorie-restricted eating plan in which people strive to consume roughly 1300 calories each day. This sort of diet is commonly used for weight loss, with calorie consumption determined by individual parameters such as age, gender, weight, exercise level, and general health goals.

The goal of a 1300 calorie diet, like all calorie-restricted diets, is to generate a calorie deficit. This signifies that the calories consumed are less than the calories expended through basal metabolic rate (BMR) and physical activity. Maintaining a calorie deficit encourages the body to burn stored fat as an energy source, resulting in weight loss.

It's crucial to note that, while calorie restriction might help you lose weight, it should be done in a healthy and balanced way. The quality of calories ingested is critical, and the diet should include a variety of nutrient-dense meals to ensure that the body gets enough vitamins, minerals, and other nutrients.

OVERVIEW OF THE 1300 CALORIE DIET

In the pursuit of a healthier lifestyle and weight control, the 1300-calorie diet develops as an organized and deliberate approach to caloric consumption. This diet is precisely planned to provide a moderate calorie deficit, enabling the body to burn stored fat for energy while still supplying important nutrients for overall health.

1. Targeted Caloric Restriction

The 1300-calorie diet is based on deliberate caloric restriction. Individuals consume roughly 1300 calories per day in order to strike a balance between maintaining a calorie deficit for weight loss and ensuring that their bodies receive the energy they require to perform efficiently.

2. Personalization and Individual Variation

While the 1300-calorie diet provides a broad framework, it is critical to consider individual differences in parameters such as age, gender, weight, and activity level. Personalization is essential for adjusting the strategy to match individual dietary needs and health goals.

3. Nutrient-Dense Food Choices: Unlike some fad diets that rely exclusively on calorie counting, the 1300-calorie diet prioritizes nutrient density. Individuals are urged to choose complete, nutrient-dense foods to meet their daily calorie needs, ensuring they get enough vitamins, minerals, and other nutrients.

4. Balanced Macronutrient Distribution: The diet promotes a well-balanced distribution of macronutrients (proteins, carbs, and fat). Striking this equilibrium is critical for maintaining energy, keeping muscle mass, and supporting overall physical processes. Proper macronutrient distribution also promotes a sense of fullness, which aids in the prevention of overeating.

5. Meal Planning and Portion Control: Successfully implementing the 1300-calorie diet requires careful meal planning and portion control. Individuals learn to prepare healthy meals within calorie limitations, making thoughtful decisions that support their nutritional goals. The goal is to develop a sustainable and joyful relationship with eating.

6. Health Benefits Beyond Weight Loss: Although weight loss is the primary goal, the 1300-calorie diet has extra health benefits. These could include improved blood sugar control, better cardiovascular health, and a lower risk of obesity-related disorders. The emphasis on nutrient-dense diets promotes general well-being.

WHO CAN BENEFIT FROM A 1300 CALORIE DIET

The 1300-calorie diet is a planned approach to calorie intake that can help some people lose weight, enhance their health, or achieve specific health goals. Here's an overview of who might benefit from a 1300-calorie diet.

1. Weight Loss Aspirants

The 1300-calorie diet can help overweight or obese individuals lose weight. The modest calorie restriction causes a deficit, causing the body to use stored fat for energy.

2. sedentary lifestyles

Sedentary individuals may benefit from the 1300-calorie diet, including office workers and desk job professionals. The reduced caloric intake corresponds to lower energy expenditure, limiting excessive calorie consumption.

3. Small or short-statured individuals

The 1300-calorie diet may be appropriate for petite individuals with lower calorie requirements. It meets their energy requirements while still supplying critical nutrients.

4. Adults with low activity levels

Seniors or people with limited mobility may benefit from a lower-calorie plan, such as the 1300-calorie diet, which aligns with their lowered energy expenditure.

5. Women With Specific Goals

Women on a Weight Loss Journey: The 1300-calorie diet can assist manage weight while providing nutritional needs.

6. Begin a Healthy Lifestyle

The 1300-calorie diet is ideal for beginners in health and nutrition, as it is simple to follow. It gradually introduces portion management and mindful eating.

7. Pre-Event or Special Occasion Preparation

Event Preparation: The 1300-calorie diet can help with short-term weight management. However, long-term sustainability must be considered.

8. Medical Conditions (under supervision)

Individuals with certain health concerns, such as metabolic disorders or obesity-related comorbidities, can use the 1300-

calorie diet for tailored management under healthcare professionals' supervision.

9. Transitioning from High Calorie Intakes

Transitioning from high-calorie diets might adopt the 1300-calorie plan to gradually reduce caloric consumption while maintaining dietary balance.

10. Athletes in the off-season or recovery

Athletes in rehabilitation may benefit from a limited caloric intake, such as the 1300-calorie diet, to avoid unwanted weight gain.

UNDERSTANDING CALORIES

Calories are the unit of measurement for energy obtained from eating. In nutritional terms, calories are the amount of energy created when the body metabolizes substances like carbs, proteins, and fats. Understanding this fundamental notion is critical for anyone beginning a nutritional journey.

Macronutrients and Caloric Content: The three major macronutrients—carbohydrates, proteins, and fats—all contribute different quantities of calories per gram. Carbohydrates and proteins each have 4 calories per gram, whereas fats have a denser 9 calories. This distinction emphasizes the significance of addressing both the quantity and quality of nutrients in a diet.

Energy Balance: The concept of energy balance revolves around the balance of calories absorbed from food and beverages and calories dissipated via metabolism and physical activity. A positive energy balance leads to weight gain, whereas a negative balance leads to weight reduction. Understanding this balance is essential for healthy weight management.

How Many Calories Do You Need

Caloric Needs Influencers: When determining an individual's daily caloric needs, several factors must be considered, including age, gender, weight, height, activity level, and overall health. The Basal Metabolic Rate (BMR) is the number of calories required by the body at rest, while Total Daily Energy Expenditure (TDEE) considers the additional calories burned during physical activity.

Calculating Caloric Requirements: To calculate caloric demands accurately, estimate BMR and adjust it based on activity levels using methods such as the Harris-Benedict equation. Online calculators and professional advice from dietitians can help you determine your personal calorie needs and create an effective food plan.

Individual Variability: It is crucial to realize that caloric requirements differ greatly amongst individuals. Muscle mass, metabolic rate, and genetic predispositions all contribute to these variances. Customizing calorie intake to individual needs is critical for achieving health and weight objectives.

CHOOSING THE RIGHT PROTEINS, CARBS, AND FATS

Proteins

Lean Protein Sources: Consuming poultry, fish, tofu, lentils, and low-fat dairy helps balance protein consumption and calorie control.

Diverse protein sources provide important amino acids needed for muscle regeneration, immunological function, and overall body upkeep.

Carbohydrates

Whole grains, fruits, vegetables, and legumes include complex carbs and fiber, which promote satiety and stable blood sugar levels.

Carbohydrate-rich foods provide critical vitamins and minerals, improving the nutritious profile of the diet.

Fats

Incorporating healthy fats like avocados, nuts, seeds, and olive oil can improve cardiovascular health and satiety.

Omega-3 and Omega-6 fatty acids, found in fatty fish, flaxseeds, and walnuts, promote brain function and regulate inflammation.

HYDRATION ROLE IN 1300 CALORIE DIET MEAL PLAN

Maintaining proper hydration is crucial for overall health and well-being, especially on a 1300-calorie diet. Water is essential for several physiological functions, including as digestion, nutrition absorption, temperature regulation, and waste removal, and Listed below are the importance of hydration.

Enhancing Weight Loss

Drinking enough water can aid weight loss attempts. Sometimes the body confuses thirst with hunger, resulting in excessive calorie consumption. Staying hydrated helps to avoid this confusion, resulting in improved appetite control and weight management.

Calorie-free Hydration

Water is a calorie-free beverage suitable for people on a calorie-restricted diet. Unlike sugary beverages, which contain empty calories, water keeps people hydrated without affecting their daily caloric intake.

Creating Hydration Ideas

1. Infused water

Add flavor to water by infusing it with fruits, herbs, or cucumber slices. This provides a pleasant twist without the extra calories or sweets found in flavored beverages.

2. Herbal teas

Use unsweetened herbal teas for a tasty and calorie-free hydration option. Whether hot or iced, herbal teas provide diversity and can be used throughout the day.

3. Hydrating Foods

Add water-rich foods like watermelon, cucumber, and celery to meals and snacks. These foods promote hydration while also delivering critical minerals and fiber.

4. Sparkling Water

Sparkling water or mineral water offers a refreshing alternative to plain water, appealing to those who crave the fizz of soda. Be aware of the extra sugars in flavored sparkling water selections.

5. Hydration reminders

Remind yourself to drink water throughout the day, especially if you tend to forget. This simple method can significantly improve hydration levels.

MEAL PLANNING

1. The importance of balance

A balanced meal is essential for achieving nutritional demands and maintaining energy levels. Each meal should have a combination of macronutrients (proteins, carbs, and fats) as well as a range of micronutrients (vitamins and minerals) to promote general health.

2. Portion Control

Controlling portion sizes is key on calorie-restricted diets like the 1300-calorie plan. Balanced portion control ensures that each food type contributes to the meal while staying within the daily caloric limit.

3. Building a plate

Separate the plate into parts for proteins, carbs, and veggies. Incorporate colorful veggies for extra vitamins and minerals, lean proteins for muscle maintenance, and complex carbohydrates for long-lasting energy.

4. Including Whole Foods

Use entire, unprocessed foods for meals. Whole grains, lean proteins, and a range of fruits and vegetables provide not just important nutrients, but also fiber, which promotes satiety and digestive health.

OVERCOMING CHALLENGES DURING 1300 CALORIE DIET PLAN

Addressing Hunger and Cravings

Understanding hunger

Knowing the difference between genuine hunger and cravings is key. True hunger is the body's signal for nourishment, whereas cravings can be prompted by external stimuli, emotions, or behaviors.

Strategies for Managing Hunger

Stay hydrated: Drinking water can reduce appetite, as the body may misinterpret thirst as hungry.

Choose nutrient-dense foods with fiber, protein, and healthy fats to promote satiety.

Eat smaller, balanced meals and snacks throughout the day to maintain constant energy levels and avoid excessive hunger.

ADDRESSING CRAVINGS

Identify causes for cravings, including stress, emotions, and specific food signals.

Choose healthier options to satisfy cravings. For example, choose dark chocolate over light chocolate.

Mindfulness Eating Practices

Use mindful eating to develop a stronger connection with food. Pay attention to flavors, textures, and feelings of fullness to create a more pleasurable eating experience.

SOCIAL AND LIFESTYLE CHALLENGES

Navigating social events

Anticipate social events and arrange accordingly. Consider eating a complete meal before attending to help manage hunger and make healthier choices.

Share your nutritional goals with friends and family to avoid pressure to break from the plan at social occasions.

Eating Outside

Before dining out, research restaurant menus online to find healthier selections that fit the 1300-calorie diet.

Practice portion management by sharing dishes or packing half the meal for later.

Travel Challenges

Pack nutritious snacks to avoid unhealthy selections during travel.

To make informed travel decisions, research local food stores and eateries in your destination.

STAYING MOTIVATED ON A 1300 CALORIE DIET

Setting realistic goals:

Set attainable short- and long-term goals. Celebrate modest achievements, such as meeting a weekly weight reduction goal or regularly adhering to the diet plan.

Creating a Support System

Share goals with friends and family for encouragement and support. A solid support network can make the journey more fun and sustainable.

Variety of Meals

Diversify your diet with different foods, flavors, and cuisines to keep it interesting. Experimenting with fresh recipes and ingredients might help to keep things interesting.

Regular Monitoring and Adjustments

Regularly monitor progress, including weight loss, energy levels, and overall health. Adjust the meal plan as needed based on your observations to guarantee continuous success.

Rewarding Progress

Create a reward system for accomplishing milestones. Non-food rewards, like a spa day or new gym gear, might help to reinforce beneficial behaviors.

Seeking professional guidance

Regularly consult with a qualified dietitian or healthcare expert for individualized guidance and adjustments to the 1300-calorie diet plan. Professional advice ensures that the nutritional plan is tailored to each individual's needs and goals.

COMMON MISTAKE TO AVOID

Skipping Meals

Skipping meals, especially on a calorie-restricted diet like the 1300-calorie plan, can cause nutritional imbalances, lower energy levels, and greater chances of overeating later in the day.

Importance of Regular Meals

Regular meals promote metabolism, stabilize blood sugar levels, and reduce appetite. Skipping meals may interrupt these processes, impeding success on the diet plan.

Strategies To Avoid

Plan meals ahead of time to maintain a regular eating routine.

Consider nutrient-dense snacks during large meal gaps.

Prioritize balanced meals that include proteins, carbs, and healthy fats.

Relying on Processed Food

Processed foods generally have extra sugars, harmful fats, and high sodium levels. Relying on these options can reduce nutritional value, impede weight loss, and contribute to health problems.

Emphasize Whole Foods

Emphasize whole, less processed foods for optimal nutritional absorption. Whole grains, lean proteins, fruits, and veggies provide critical vitamins, minerals, and fiber without any unneeded additions.

Reading Labels

Always read food labels. Avoid items with high sugar content, artificial preservatives, and unidentifiable substances.

Cooking At Home

Choose homemade meals for more control over ingredients and cooking methods. This provides for more nutritious meal options and portion control.

Disregarding Individual Nutritional Needs

Nutritional demands vary depending on age, gender, activity level, and health state. Ignoring these specific requirements can result in nutritional imbalances and impede progress.

Importance of Personalization

Adjust the 1300-calorie diet to meet individual preferences and needs. Consider working with a licensed dietitian to develop a personalized plan that corresponds with your individual health goals.

Balancing macronutrients

Balance macronutrients (proteins, carbs, and fats) according to individual needs. Neglecting one category can have an influence on your energy, satiety, and overall well-being.

Regular Monitoring and Adjustments

Monitor progress and alter diet accordingly. Changes in weight, energy levels, or health status may suggest that changes are required to meet individual nutritional requirements.

CHAPTER 1

Breakfast Recipes

1. Greek Yogurt Parfait with Berries and Almonds

Health Benefits

- Greek yogurt provides protein and probiotics for gut health.
- Berries offer antioxidants and vitamins.
- Almonds contribute healthy fats and additional protein.

Ingredients

- 1 cup Greek yogurt
- Mixed berries (strawberries, blueberries, raspberries) of 1/2 cup
- 2 tablespoons almonds, sliced
- 1 tablespoon honey or maple syrup

Mode of Preparation

- Greek yogurt should be layered with mixed berries in a glass or bowl.
- Top with sliced almonds and drizzle with honey or maple syrup.

Nutritional Information (Per Serving)

- **Calories:** Approx. 250
- **Protein:** Approx. 20g
- **Carbohydrates:** Approx. 25g
- **Fiber:** Approx. 4g
- **Total Fat:** Approx. 10g

Serving Size: 1 serving.

Cooking Time: 5 minutes.

Preparation Time: 5 minutes.

2. Vegetable Omelette with Whole Wheat Toast

Health Benefits

- Eggs provide high-quality protein.
- Vegetables offer vitamins and fiber.
- Whole wheat toast adds complex carbohydrates.

Ingredients

- 2 large eggs
- 1/2 cup bell peppers, diced
- 1/4 cup onion, diced
- 1/4 cup spinach, chopped
- 1 teaspoon olive oil
- Salt and pepper to taste
- 2 slices whole wheat bread

Mode of Preparation

- Eggs should be Whisked and season with salt and pepper.
- Sauté vegetables in olive oil until softened.

- Pour eggs over vegetables, cook until set, and fold into an omelette.
- Toast whole wheat bread slices.

Nutritional Information (Per Serving)

- **Calories:** Approx. 320
- **Protein:** Approx. 20g
- **Carbohydrates:** Approx. 30g
- **Fiber:** Approx. 6g
- **Total Fat:** Approx. 15g

Serving Size: 1 omelette with 2 slices of toast.

Cooking Time: 10 minutes.

Preparation Time: 10 minutes.

3. Overnight Chia Seed Pudding

Health Benefits

- Chia seeds is said to give omega-3 fatty acids and fiber.
- Dairy or plant-based milk offers calcium.
- Berries add antioxidants and natural sweetness.

Ingredients

- 3 tablespoons chia seeds
- 1 cup milk (dairy or plant-based)
- 1/2 teaspoon vanilla extract
- 1 tablespoon honey or maple syrup
- 1/2 cup mixed berries (strawberries, blueberries)

Mode of Preparation

- Mix chia seeds, milk, vanilla extract, and sweetener in a jar.
- It should be Refrigerated overnight or for at least 4 hours.

- Top with mixed berries before serving.

Nutritional Information (Per Serving)

- **Calories:** Approx. 280
- **Protein:** Approx. 10g
- **Carbohydrates:** Approx. 30g
- **Fiber:** Approx. 12g
- **Total Fat:** Approx. 14g

Serving Size: 1 serving.

Preparation Time: 5 minutes (plus chilling time).

4. Avocado and Egg Toast

Health Benefits

- Avocado provides healthy fats and fiber.
- Eggs offer protein.
- Whole grain bread adds complex carbohydrates.

Ingredients

- 1 slice whole grain bread
- 1/2 avocado, mashed

- 1 poached or fried egg
- Salt
- Chili flakes
- Pepper

Mode of Preparation

- Toast the whole grain bread.
- Spread mashed avocado on the toast.
- Top with a poached or fried egg.
- It should be seasoned with salt, pepper, and chili flakes.

Nutritional Information (Per Serving)

- **Calories:** Approx. 300
- **Protein:** Approx. 12g
- **Carbohydrates:** Approx. 20g
- **Fiber:** Approx. 8g
- **Total Fat:** Approx. 20g

Serving Size: 1 serving.

Cooking Time: 10 minutes.

Preparation Time: 5 minutes.

5. Berry and Spinach Smoothie Bowl
Health Benefits

- Berries are rich in antioxidants and vitamins.
- Spinach adds iron and additional vitamins.
- Greek yogurt provides protein and probiotics.

Ingredients

- Mixed berries (strawberries, blueberries, raspberries) of 1/2 cup
- 1 cup spinach
- 1/2 banana, frozen
- 1/2 cup Greek yogurt
- 1/2 cup almond milk
- Toppings: granola, sliced banana, chia seeds

Mode of Preparation

- Blend berries, spinach, frozen banana, Greek yogurt, and almond milk until smooth.
- Pour into a bowl and top with granola, sliced banana, and chia seeds.

Nutritional Information (Per Serving)

- **Calories:** Approx. 280
- **Protein:** Approx. 15g
- **Carbohydrates:** Approx. 35g
- **Fiber:** Approx. 8g
- **Total Fat:** Approx. 10g

Serving Size: 1 bowl.

Preparation Time: 5 minutes.

6. Whole Grain Pancakes with Mixed Berries
Health Benefits

- Whole grains provide complex carbohydrates.
- Mixed berries offer antioxidants and vitamins.
- Greek yogurt adds protein and creaminess.

Ingredients

- 1/2 cup whole wheat flour
- 1/2 cup oats, ground into flour
- 1 teaspoon baking powder
- 1/2 cup Greek yogurt
- 1/2 cup milk (dairy or plant-based)
- 1 egg
- 1 tablespoon honey or maple syrup
- Mixed berries for topping

Mode of Preparation

- Mix whole wheat flour, ground oats, baking powder, Greek yogurt, milk, egg, and sweetener until well combined.
- Cook pancakes on a griddle or pan.
- Top with mixed berries.

Nutritional Information (Per Serving)

- **Calories:** Approx. 350
- **Protein:** Approx. 15g
- **Carbohydrates:** Approx. 50g
- **Fiber:** Approx. 8g
- **Total Fat:** Approx. 10g

Serving Size: 2-3 pancakes.

Cooking Time: 15 minutes.

Preparation Time: 10 minutes.

7. Spinach and Feta Breakfast Wrap

Health Benefits

- Spinach provides iron and vitamins.
- Feta adds flavor with fewer calories.
- Whole grain wrap offers complex carbs.

Ingredients

- 1 whole grain wrap
- 2 eggs, scrambled
- 1 cup fresh spinach
- 2 tablespoons feta cheese, crumbled
- Salt and pepper to taste

Mode of Preparation

- Sauté fresh spinach until wilted.
- Scramble eggs and mix with sautéed spinach.
- Place the mixture in a whole grain wrap, sprinkle with feta, and season with salt and pepper.

Nutritional Information (Per Serving)

- **Calories:** Approx. 320
- **Protein:** Approx. 20g
- **Carbohydrates:** Approx. 25g
- **Fiber:** Approx. 5g
- **Total Fat:** Approx. 15g

Serving Size: 1 wrap.

Cooking Time: 10 minutes.

Preparation Time: 10 minutes.

8. Protein-Packed Berry Smoothie

Health Benefits

- Protein powder adds extra protein for muscle health.
- Berries provide antioxidants and vitamins.
- Almond milk adds creaminess with fewer calories.

Ingredients

- Mixed berries (strawberries, blueberries, raspberries) of 1/2 cup
- 1 scoop protein powder (whey or plant-based)
- 1 cup almond milk
- 1/2 banana, frozen
- 1 tablespoon almond butter
- Ice cubes (optional)

Mode of Preparation

- Blend mixed berries, protein powder, almond milk, frozen banana, and almond butter until smooth.
- Add ice cubes if desired.

Nutritional Information (Per Serving)

- **Calories:** Approx. 300
- **Protein:** Approx. 25g
- **Carbohydrates:** Approx. 30g
- **Fiber:** Approx. 7g
- **Total Fat:** Approx. 12g

Serving Size: 1 smoothie.

Preparation Time: 5 minutes.

9. Egg White and Vegetable Scramble
Health Benefits

- Egg whites provide protein with fewer calories.
- Colorful vegetables offer vitamins and fiber.
- Avocado adds healthy fats.

Ingredients

- 1 cup egg whites
- 1/2 cup bell peppers, diced
- 1/4 cup cherry tomatoes, halved

- 1/4 cup spinach, chopped
- 1/4 avocado, sliced
- Salt and pepper to taste

Mode of Preparation

- Sauté bell peppers until slightly softened.
- Add cherry tomatoes and spinach, cook until wilted.
- Pour in egg whites, cook until set, and season with salt and pepper.
- Serve with sliced avocado.

Nutritional Information (Per Serving)

- **Calories:** Approx. 280
- **Protein:** Approx. 30g
- **Carbohydrates:** Approx. 15g
- **Fiber:** Approx. 5g
- **Total Fat:** Approx. 12g

Serving Size: 1 serving.

Cooking Time: 10 minutes.

Preparation Time: 10 minutes.

10. Cottage Cheese and Pineapple Bowl
Health Benefits

- Cottage cheese is rich in protein and low in calories.
- Pineapple provides vitamins and natural sweetness.
- Walnuts add healthy fats.

Ingredients

- 1 cup low-fat cottage cheese
- 1 cup fresh pineapple chunks
- 2 tablespoons walnuts, chopped
- 1 tablespoon honey

Mode of Preparation

- Cottage cheese should be mixed with fresh pineapple chunks.

- Sprinkle chopped walnuts on top and drizzle with honey.

Nutritional Information (Per Serving)

- **Calories:** Approx. 300
- **Protein:** Approx. 25g
- **Carbohydrates:** Approx. 30g
- **Fiber:** Approx. 3g
- **Total Fat:** Approx. 10g

Serving Size: 1 bowl.

Preparation Time: 5 minutes.

11. Oatmeal with Banana and Almond Butter

Health Benefits

- Oats provide soluble fiber for heart health.
- Bananas offer potassium and natural sweetness.
- Almond butter provides with healthy fats and protein.

Ingredients

- 1/2 cup rolled oats
- Water or milk (dairy or plant-based) of 1 cup
- 1/2 banana, sliced
- 1 tablespoon almond butter
- Cinnamon and honey for flavor (optional)

Mode of Preparation

- Cook oats with water or milk until creamy.
- Top with sliced banana, almond butter, and optional cinnamon and honey.

Nutritional Information (Per Serving)

- **Calories:** Approx. 300
- **Protein:** Approx. 10g
- **Carbohydrates:** Approx. 45g
- **Fiber:** Approx. 7g
- **Total Fat:** Approx. 10g

Serving Size: 1 bowl.

Cooking Time: 5 minutes.

Preparation Time: 5 minutes.

12. Smoked Salmon and Cream Cheese Bagel

Health Benefits

- Smoked salmon provides omega-3 fatty acids and protein.
- Whole grain bagel adds complex carbs.
- Cream cheese contributes creaminess and flavor.

Ingredients

- 1 whole grain bagel
- 2 oz smoked salmon
- 2 tablespoons cream cheese
- Red onion slices, capers, and dill for garnish

Mode of Preparation

- Toast the whole grain bagel.
- Spread cream cheese on each half.
- It should be topped with smoked salmon, red onion slices, capers, and dill.

Nutritional Information (Per Serving)

- **Calories:** Approx. 350
- **Protein:** Approx. 20g
- **Carbohydrates:** Approx. 30g
- **Fiber:** Approx. 5g
- **Total Fat:** Approx. 15g

Serving Size: 1 bagel.

Preparation Time: 5 minutes.

13. Peanut Butter and Banana Smoothie

Health Benefits

- Peanut butter provides protein and healthy fats.
- Bananas provide potassium and natural sweetness.
- Greek yogurt supplies creaminess and additional protein.

Ingredients

- 1 banana
- 2 tablespoons peanut butter

- 1/2 cup Greek yogurt
- 1 cup milk (dairy or plant-based)
- Ice cubes (optional)

Mode of Preparation

- Blend banana, peanut butter, Greek yogurt, and milk until smooth.
- Add ice cubes if desired.

Nutritional Information (Per Serving)

- **Calories:** Approx. 350
- **Protein:** Approx. 15g
- **Carbohydrates:** Approx. 30g
- **Fiber:** Approx. 5g
- **Total Fat:** Approx. 20g

Serving Size: 1 smoothie.

Preparation Time: 5 minutes.

14. Vegetarian Breakfast Burrito

Health Benefits

- Eggs provide high-quality protein.
- Black beans support with plant-based protein and fiber.
- Avocado adds healthy fats and creaminess.

Ingredients

- 2 large eggs, scrambled
- 1/2 cup black beans, cooked
- 1/4 cup diced tomatoes
- 1/4 cup diced bell peppers
- 1/4 avocado, sliced
- Whole wheat tortilla

Mode of Preparation

- Scramble eggs until cooked through.
- Warm the tortilla and fill with scrambled eggs, black beans, tomatoes, bell peppers, and avocado.

Nutritional Information (Per Serving)

- **Calories:** Approx. 320
- **Protein:** Approx. 20g
- **Carbohydrates:** Approx. 30g
- **Fiber:** Approx. 8g
- **Total Fat:** Approx. 15g

Serving Size: 1 burrito.

Cooking Time: 10 minutes.

Preparation Time: 10 minutes.

15. Cinnamon Apple Quinoa Bowl

Health Benefits

- Quinoa provides complete proteins and essential amino acids.
- Apples offer fiber and natural sweetness.
- Cinnamon adds flavor without extra calories.

Ingredients

- 1/2 cup cooked quinoa
- 1 apple, diced
- 1/2 teaspoon cinnamon
- 1 tablespoon almond butter
- Chopped nuts for topping (optional)

Mode of Preparation

- Mix cooked quinoa with diced apples.
- Sprinkle with cinnamon and drizzle with almond butter.
- Top with chopped nuts if desired.

Nutritional Information (Per Serving)

- **Calories:** Approx. 300
- **Protein:** Approx. 8g
- **Carbohydrates:** Approx. 40g
- **Fiber:** Approx. 7g
- **Total Fat:** Approx. 12g

Serving Size: 1 bowl.

Cooking Time: 15 minutes.

Preparation Time: 5 minutes.

16. Chia Seed and Berry Smoothie

Health Benefits

- Chia seeds gives omega-3 fatty acids and fiber.
- Berries offer antioxidants and vitamins.
- Greek yogurt adds protein and creaminess.

Ingredients

- 2 tablespoons chia seeds

- Mixed berries (strawberries, blueberries, raspberries) of 1/2 cup
- 1/2 cup Greek yogurt
- 1 cup almond milk
- 1 tablespoon honey or maple syrup
- Ice cubes (optional)

Mode of Preparation

- Blend chia seeds, mixed berries, Greek yogurt, almond milk, and sweetener until smooth.
- Add ice cubes if desired.

Nutritional Information (Per Serving)

- **Calories:** Approx. 280
- **Protein:** Approx. 10g
- **Carbohydrates:** Approx. 30g
- **Fiber:** Approx. 12g
- **Total Fat:** Approx. 14g

Serving Size 1 smoothie.

Preparation Time: 5 minutes.

17. Turkey and Vegetable Breakfast Wrap
Health Benefits

- Lean protein from turkey.
- Vegetables provide vitamins and minerals.
- Whole grain wrap adds fiber for satiety.

Ingredients

- 4 oz ground turkey, cooked
- 1 whole-grain wrap
- 1/4 cup black beans, cooked
- 1/4 cup diced tomatoes
- 1/4 cup bell peppers, diced
- 1/4 cup shredded cheese
- 1 tablespoon salsa

Mode of Preparation

- Cook ground turkey until browned.

- Warm the whole grain wrap and fill with cooked turkey, black beans, tomatoes, bell peppers, shredded cheese, and salsa.

Nutritional Information (Per Serving)

- **Calories:** Approx. 330

- **Protein:** Approx. 25g

- **Carbohydrates:** Approx. 30g

- **Fiber:** Approx. 8g

- **Total Fat:** Approx. 15g

Serving Size: 1 wrap.

Cooking Time: 15 minutes.

Preparation Time: 10 minutes.

18. Cottage Cheese Pancakes

Health Benefits

- Cottage cheese provides protein and calcium.
- Whole grain flour adds fiber.
- Berries offer antioxidants.

Ingredients

- 1/2 cup low-fat cottage cheese
- 1/2 cup whole wheat flour
- 1 egg
- 1/2 teaspoon baking powder
- 1/2 cup mixed berries
- Greek yogurt for topping

Mode of Preparation

- Blend cottage cheese, whole wheat flour, egg, and baking powder until smooth.
- Cook pancakes on a griddle.
- Top with mixed berries and a dollop of Greek yogurt.

Nutritional Information (Per Serving)

- **Calories:** Approx. 320
- **Protein:** Approx. 20g
- **Carbohydrates:** Approx. 35g
- **Fiber:** Approx. 6g
- **Total Fat:** Approx. 10g

Serving Size: 2-3 pancakes.

Cooking Time: 15 minutes.

Preparation Time: 10 minutes.

19. Mushroom and Spinach Scramble

Health Benefits

- Mushrooms and spinach provide vitamins and minerals.
- Eggs offer protein and essential nutrients.
- Whole grain toast adds complex carbs.

Ingredients

- 2 eggs, scrambled

- 1/2 cup mushrooms, sliced
- 1 cup spinach, chopped
- 1 teaspoon olive oil
- Salt and pepper to taste
- 2 slices whole grain bread

Mode of Preparation

- Sauté mushrooms in olive oil until browned.
- Add chopped spinach and cook until wilted.
- Scramble eggs and mix with mushrooms and spinach.
- Serve with whole grain toast.

Nutritional Information (Per Serving)

- **Calories:** Approx. 340
- **Protein:** Approx. 20g
- **Carbohydrates:** Approx. 30g
- **Fiber:** Approx. 7g
- **Total Fat:** Approx. 15g

Serving Size: 1 serving.

Cooking Time 10 minutes.

Preparation Time: 10 minutes.

20. Blueberry Almond Overnight Oats
Health Benefits

- Oats provide fiber for digestive health.
- Blueberries offer antioxidants and vitamins.
- Almonds add healthy fats and crunch.

Ingredients

- 1/2 cup rolled oats
- 1/2 cup almond milk
- 1/4 cup blueberries
- 1 tablespoon almond butter
- 1 teaspoon honey
- Sliced almonds for topping

Mode of Preparation

- Mix rolled oats, almond milk, blueberries, almond butter, and honey in a jar.
- Refrigerate overnight.
- Top with sliced almonds before serving.

Nutritional Information (Per Serving)

- **Calories:** Approx. 300
- **Protein:** Approx. 10g
- **Carbohydrates:** Approx. 40g
- **Fiber:** Approx. 8g
- **Total Fat:** Approx. 12g

Serving Size: 1 serving.

Preparation Time: 5 minutes (plus chilling time).

CHAPTER 2

Lunch Recipes

1. Quinoa and Vegetable Power Bow
Health Benefits

- Quinoa provides complete proteins and essential amino acids.
- Assorted vegetables offer a spectrum of vitamins and minerals.
- Avocado contributes healthy fats and promotes satiety.

Ingredients

- 1/2 cup quinoa (uncooked)
- 1 cup broccoli florets
- 1/2 cup cherry tomatoes, halved
- 1/2 cup cucumber, diced
- 1/4 cup red bell pepper, diced
- 1/4 cup feta cheese, crumbled

- 1/4 avocado, sliced
- 2 tablespoons olive oil
- Juice of half a lemon
- Salt and pepper to taste

Mode of Preparation

1. Cook quinoa according to package instructions.
2. Steam broccoli until tender-crisp.
3. In a bowl, combine cooked quinoa, broccoli, cherry tomatoes, cucumber, red bell pepper, feta cheese, and avocado slices.
4. In a separate small bowl, whisk together olive oil, lemon juice, salt, and pepper. Drizzle over the bowl and toss to combine.

Nutritional Information (Per Serving)

- **Calories:** Approx. 380
- **Protein:** Approx. 12g
- **Carbohydrates:** Approx. 40g

- **Fiber:** Approx. 8g
- **Total Fat:** Approx. 20g

Serving Size: 1 bowl.

Cooking Time: 25 minutes.

Preparation Time: 15 minutes.

2. Turkey and Veggie Stir-Fry
Health Benefits

- Lean protein from turkey supports muscle health.
- Vegetables gives essential vitamins and minerals.
- Stir-frying preserves nutrients and keeps the dish low in added fats.

Ingredients

- 4 oz lean ground turkey
- 1 cup broccoli florets
- 1/2 cup snap peas
- 1/2 cup carrots, thinly sliced
- 1/4 cup low-sodium soy sauce

- 1 tablespoon sesame oil
- 1 tablespoon ginger, minced
- 2 cloves garlic, minced
- 2 green onions, sliced
- 1 tablespoon olive oil (for cooking)

Mode of Preparation

1. Olive oil should be heated in a large skillet over medium heat.
2. Add ground turkey and cook until browned.
3. Add broccoli, snap peas, and carrots. Stir-fry until vegetables are tender-crisp.
4. In a small bowl, mix soy sauce, sesame oil, ginger, and garlic. Pour over the turkey and vegetables, tossing to coat.
5. Garnish with sliced green onions.

Nutritional Information (Per Serving)

- **Calories:** Approx. 330
- **Protein:** Approx. 25g
- **Carbohydrates:** Approx. 20g
- **Fiber:** Approx. 5g
- **Total Fat:** Approx. 18g

Serving Size: 1 plate.

Cooking Time: 20 minutes.

Preparation Time: 15 minutes.

3. Salmon and Quinoa Stuffed Bell Peppers

Health Benefits

- Omega-3 fatty acids from salmon promote heart health.
- Quinoa gives a complete source of protein.
- Bell peppers offer vitamins and antioxidants.

Ingredients

- 2 bell peppers, halved and seeds removed

- 8 oz salmon fillet, cooked and flaked
- 1/2 cup quinoa (uncooked)
- 1/4 cup red onion, finely chopped
- 1/4 cup cherry tomatoes, diced
- 1/4 cup feta cheese, crumbled
- 1 tablespoon olive oil
- Juice of half a lemon
- 1 teaspoon dried oregano
- Salt and pepper to taste

Mode of Preparation

1. Preheat the oven to 375°F (190°C).
2. Cook quinoa according to package instructions.
3. In a bowl, combine flaked salmon, cooked quinoa, red onion, cherry tomatoes, feta cheese, olive oil, lemon juice, oregano, salt, and pepper.
4. Stuff the bell pepper halves with the mixture.

5. Bake for 20-25 minutes or until the peppers are tender.

Nutritional Information (Per Serving)

- **Calories:** Approx. 400
- **Protein:** Approx. 30g
- **Carbohydrates:** Approx. 30g
- **Fiber:** Approx. 5g
- **Total Fat:** Approx. 18g

Serving Size: 2 stuffed bell pepper halves.

Cooking Time: 30 minutes.

Preparation Time: 20 minutes.

4. Mediterranean Chickpea Wrap

Health Benefits

- Chickpeas provide plant-based protein and fiber.
- Vegetables offer vitamins and minerals.
- Olive oil contributes heart-healthy monounsaturated fats.

Ingredients

- 1 whole-grain wrap
- 1 cup chickpeas (canned, drained, and rinsed)
- 1/2 cup cucumber, diced
- 1/4 cup cherry tomatoes, halved
- 1/4 cup red bell pepper, diced
- 2 tablespoons feta cheese, crumbled
- 1 tablespoon Kalamata olives, sliced
- 1 tablespoon olive oil
- Juice of half a lemon
- 1 teaspoon dried oregano

- Salt and pepper to taste

Mode of Preparation

1. In a bowl, combine chickpeas, cucumber, cherry tomatoes, red bell pepper, feta cheese, olives, olive oil, lemon juice, oregano, salt, and pepper.

2. Warm the whole-grain wrap.

3. Spoon the chickpea mixture onto the wrap.

4. Roll the wrap tightly.

Nutritional Information (Per Serving)

- **Calories:** Approx. 350
- **Protein:** Approx. 15g
- **Carbohydrates:** Approx. 45g
- **Fiber:** Approx. 10g
- **Total Fat:** Approx. 15g

Serving Size: 1 wrap.

Cooking Time: 10 minutes.

Preparation Time: 15 minutes.

5. Tofu and Vegetable Stir-Fry with Brown Rice
Health Benefits

- Tofu provides plant-based protein and is low in saturated fats.
- Brown rice offers complex carbohydrates and dietary fiber.
- Assorted vegetables provide essential nutrients.

Ingredients

- 1/2 cup brown rice (uncooked)
- 6 oz firm tofu, cubed
- 1 cup broccoli florets
- 1/2 cup carrots, thinly sliced
- 1/2 cup snap peas
- 1/4 cup low-sodium soy sauce
- 1 tablespoon sesame oil
- 1 tablespoon ginger, minced
- 2 cloves garlic, minced

- 1 tablespoon olive oil (for cooking)

Mode of Preparation

1. Cook brown rice according to package instructions.
2. Olive oil should be heated in a large skillet over medium heat.
3. Add tofu cubes and stir-fry until golden brown.
4. Add broccoli, carrots, and snap peas. Stir-fry until vegetables are tender-crisp.
5. In a small bowl, mix soy sauce, sesame oil, ginger, and garlic. Pour over the tofu and vegetables. Toss to coat.
6. Serve over cooked brown rice.

Nutritional Information (Per Serving)

- **Calories:** Approx. 380
- **Protein:** Approx. 20g
- **Carbohydrates:** Approx. 50g
- **Fiber:** Approx. 8g

- **Total Fat:** Approx. 15g

Serving Size: 1 plate.

Cooking Time: 25 minutes.

Preparation Time: 20 minutes.

6. Chickpea and Spinach Salad with Lemon-Tahini Dressing
Health Benefits

- Chickpeas provide plant-based protein and fiber.
- Spinach is very good in iron and vitamins supply.
- Tahini dressing offers healthy fats and adds a flavorful kick.

Ingredients

- Canned chickpeas, drained and rinsed of 1 cup
- 2 cups fresh spinach leaves
- 1/2 cup cherry tomatoes, halved
- 1/4 cup red onion, thinly sliced
- 2 tablespoons tahini

- Juice of one lemon
- 1 tablespoon olive oil
- Salt and pepper to taste

Mode of Preparation

1. In a large bowl, combine chickpeas, spinach, cherry tomatoes, and red onion.
2. In a small bowl, whisk together tahini, lemon juice, olive oil, salt, and pepper.
3. The dressing should be drizzled over the salad and toss gently to coat.

Nutritional Information (Per Serving)

- **Calories:** Approx. 320
- **Protein:** Approx. 12g
- **Carbohydrates:** Approx. 40g
- **Fiber:** Approx. 10g
- **Total Fat:** Approx. 15g

Serving Size: 1 bowl.
Cooking Time: 15 minutes.
Preparation Time: 10 minutes.

7. Shrimp and Avocado Wrap

Health Benefits

- Shrimp provides lean protein with low-calorie content.
- Avocado offers healthy fats and a creamy texture.
- Whole-grain wrap adds fiber for satiety.

Ingredients

- 4 oz shrimp, cooked and peeled
- 1 whole-grain wrap
- 1/2 avocado, sliced
- 1/4 cup shredded lettuce
- 1/4 cup cucumber, julienned
- 1/4 cup mango, diced (optional)
- 1 tablespoon Greek yogurt
- Juice of half a lime
- Salt and pepper to taste

Mode of Preparation

1. In a bowl, mix cooked shrimp with Greek yogurt, lime juice, salt, and pepper.

2. Warm the whole-grain wrap.

3. Assemble the wrap with shrimp mixture, avocado slices, shredded lettuce, cucumber, and mango if desired.

4. Roll the wrap tightly.

Nutritional Information (Per Serving)

- **Calories:** Approx. 340
- **Protein:** Approx. 25g
- **Carbohydrates:** Approx. 30g
- **Fiber:** Approx. 8g
- **Total Fat:** Approx. 15g

Serving Size: 1 wrap.

Cooking Time: 10 minutes.

Preparation Time: 15 minutes.

8. Egg and Vegetable Stir-Fry with Quinoa
Health Benefits

- Eggs provide high-quality protein and essential amino acids.
- Vegetables gives a variety of nutrients.
- Quinoa adds complex carbohydrates and fiber.

Ingredients

- 2 large eggs, beaten
- 1/2 cup quinoa (uncooked)
- Mixed vegetables (bell peppers, peas, carrots) of 1 cup
- 1/4 cup green onions, chopped
- 1 tablespoon soy sauce
- 1 tablespoon sesame oil
- 1 teaspoon ginger, minced
- 2 cloves garlic, minced
- 1 tablespoon olive oil (for cooking)

Mode of Preparation

1. Cook quinoa according to package instructions.
2. Olive oil should be heated in a large skillet over medium heat.
3. Beaten eggs and scramble should be added until cooked.
4. Add mixed vegetables, soy sauce, sesame oil, ginger, and garlic. Stir-fry until vegetables are tender.
5. Mix in cooked quinoa and green onions.

Nutritional Information (Per Serving)

- **Calories:** Approx. 360
- **Protein:** Approx. 18g
- **Carbohydrates:** Approx. 35g
- **Fiber:** Approx. 6g
- **Total Fat:** Approx. 18g

Serving Size: 1 plate.

Cooking Time: 20 minutes.

Preparation Time: 15 minutes.

9. Black Bean and Vegetable Burrito Bowl
Health Benefits

- Black beans gives plant-based protein and fiber.
- Brown rice offers complex carbohydrates.
- Assorted vegetables contribute essential vitamins and minerals.

Ingredients

- 1/2 cup brown rice (uncooked)
- 1 cup black beans (canned, drained, and rinsed)
- 1/2 cup corn kernels
- 1/4 cup red onion, diced
- 1/4 cup bell peppers, diced
- 1/4 cup salsa
- 1/4 cup Greek yogurt
- Fresh cilantro, chopped (for garnish)
- Lime wedges (optional)

Mode of Preparation

1. Cook brown rice according to package instructions.
2. In a bowl, combine cooked rice, black beans, corn, red onion, bell peppers, salsa, and Greek yogurt.
3. Mix well and garnish with fresh cilantro.
4. Serve with lime wedges if desired.

Nutritional Information (Per Serving)

- **Calories:** Approx. 340
- **Protein:** Approx. 15g
- **Carbohydrates:** Approx. 60g
- **Fiber:** Approx. 10g
- **Total Fat:** Approx. 5g

Serving Size: 1 bowl.

Cooking Time: 25 minutes.

Preparation Time: 15 minutes.

10. Caprese Salad with Grilled Chicken

Health Benefits

- Grilled chicken provides lean protein.
- Tomatoes offer antioxidants, vitamins, and minerals.
- Fresh mozzarella adds a creamy texture and calcium.

Ingredients

- 4 oz grilled chicken breast, sliced
- 1 cup cherry tomatoes, halved
- 1/2 cup fresh mozzarella balls
- Fresh basil leaves
- 1 tablespoon balsamic glaze
- 1 tablespoon olive oil
- Salt and pepper to taste

Mode of Preparation

1. Grill chicken until cooked through and slice.
2. In a bowl, combine sliced chicken, cherry tomatoes, fresh mozzarella balls, and fresh basil leaves.

3. Drizzle with olive oil and balsamic glaze.

4. Season with salt and pepper.

Nutritional Information (Per Serving)

- **Calories:** Approx. 350
- **Protein:** Approx. 30g
- **Carbohydrates:** Approx. 10g
- **Fiber:** Approx. 2g
- **Total Fat:** Approx. 20g

Serving Size: 1 plate.

Cooking Time: 15 minutes.

Preparation Time: 10 minutes.

11. Mango and Shrimp Quinoa Salad
Health Benefits

- Shrimp provides lean protein with low-calorie content.
- Quinoa offers complete proteins and dietary fiber.
- Mango adds natural sweetness and vitamins.

Ingredients

- 1/2 cup quinoa (uncooked)
- 4 oz shrimp, cooked and peeled
- 1/2 cup mango, diced
- 1/4 cup red bell pepper, diced
- 1/4 cup cucumber, diced
- 2 tablespoons cilantro, chopped
- 1 tablespoon olive oil
- Juice of one lime
- Salt and pepper to taste

Mode of Preparation

1. Cook quinoa according to package instructions.

2. In a bowl, combine cooked quinoa, shrimp, mango, red bell pepper, cucumber, and cilantro.

3. In a separate small bowl, whisk together olive oil, lime juice, salt, and pepper.

4. It should be Drizzled over the salad and toss gently to combine.

Nutritional Information (Per Serving)

- **Calories:** Approx. 340
- **Protein:** Approx. 20g
- **Carbohydrates:** Approx. 40g
- **Fiber:** Approx. 5g
- **Total Fat:** Approx. 12g

Serving Size: 1 bowl.

Cooking Time: 20 minutes.

Preparation Time: 15 minutes.

12. Chicken and Vegetable Brown Rice Bowl

Health Benefits

- Chicken provides lean protein for muscle health.
- Brown rice offers complex carbohydrates and dietary fiber.
- Mixed vegetables add vitamins and minerals.

Ingredients

- 1/2 cup brown rice (uncooked)
- 4 oz chicken breast, grilled and sliced
- 1/2 cup broccoli florets
- 1/2 cup carrots, julienned
- 1/2 cup snow peas
- 1 tablespoon low-sodium soy sauce
- 1 tablespoon sesame oil
- 1 tablespoon green onions, sliced
- 1 teaspoon sesame seeds (for garnish)

Mode of Preparation

1. Cook brown rice according to package instructions.
2. Sesame oil should be heated over medium heat in a large skillet,.
3. Add grilled chicken, broccoli, carrots, and snow peas. Stir-fry until vegetables are tender.
4. Stir in soy sauce and green onions.
5. Serve the chicken and vegetables over cooked brown rice, garnished with sesame seeds.

Nutritional Information (Per Serving)

- **Calories:** Approx. 380
- **Protein:** Approx. 25g
- **Carbohydrates:** Approx. 45g
- **Fiber:** Approx. 6g
- **Total Fat:** Approx. 12g

Serving Size: 1 bowl.

Cooking Time: 25 minutes.

Preparation Time: 20 minutes.

13. Spinach and Feta Stuffed Chicken Breast

Health Benefits

- Chicken breast provides lean protein.
- Spinach offers vitamins and iron.
- Feta cheese adds a flavorful touch with moderate fat content.

Ingredients

- 2 boneless, skinless chicken breasts
- 1 cup fresh spinach leaves
- 1/4 cup feta cheese, crumbled
- 1 tablespoon olive oil
- 1 teaspoon garlic powder
- 1 teaspoon dried oregano
- Salt and pepper to taste

Mode of Preparation

1. Preheat the oven to 375°F (190°C).

2. Butterfly the chicken breasts to create a pocket.

3. In a bowl, mix together fresh spinach, feta cheese, olive oil, garlic powder, oregano, salt, and pepper.

4. Stuff the chicken breasts with the spinach and feta mixture.

5. It should be baked for 25-30 minutes or until the chicken is cooked through.

Nutritional Information (Per Serving)

- **Calories:** Approx. 320
- **Protein:** Approx. 35g
- **Carbohydrates:** Approx. 3g
- **Fiber:** Approx. 1g
- **Total Fat:** Approx. 18g

Serving Size: 1 stuffed chicken breast.

Cooking Time: 30 minutes.

Preparation Time: 15 minutes.

14. Vegetarian Lentil and Sweet Potato Chili

Health Benefits

- Lentils provide plant-based protein and fiber.
- Sweet potatoes offer complex carbohydrates and vitamins.
- Chili spices may boost metabolism and have anti-inflammatory properties.

Ingredients

- Dry green or brown lentils, rinsed of 1 cup
- 1 large sweet potato, diced
- 1 can (15 oz) diced tomatoes
- Black beans, drained and rinsed of 1 can (15 oz)
- 1 cup vegetable broth
- 1 onion, diced
- 2 cloves garlic, minced
- 1 tablespoon chili powder
- 1 teaspoon cumin

- 1/2 teaspoon smoked paprika
- Salt and pepper to taste
- 1 tablespoon olive oil

Mode of Preparation

1. Olive oil should be heated over medium heat in a large pot.
2. Sauté onion and garlic until softened.
3. Add sweet potatoes, lentils, diced tomatoes, black beans, vegetable broth, chili powder, cumin, smoked paprika, salt, and pepper.
4. Bring to a boil, then reduce heat and simmer for 25-30 minutes or until lentils and sweet potatoes are tender.

Nutritional Information (Per Serving)

- **Calories:** Approx. 350
- **Protein:** Approx. 20g
- **Carbohydrates:** Approx. 60g
- **Fiber:** Approx. 15g

- **Total Fat:** Approx. 5g

Serving Size: 1 bowl.

Cooking Time: 30 minutes.

Preparation Time: 20 minutes.

15. Turkey and Quinoa Stuffed Bell Peppers
Health Benefits

- Lean turkey provides protein with less saturated fat.
- Quinoa offers complete proteins and dietary fiber.
- Bell peppers provide vitamins and antioxidants.

Ingredients

- 4 large bell peppers, halved and seeds removed
- 1/2 cup quinoa (uncooked)
- 1 lb lean ground turkey
- Diced tomatoes, drained of 1 can (15 oz)
- 1/2 cup black beans, drained and rinsed
- 1/2 cup corn kernels

- 1 teaspoon cumin
- 1 teaspoon chili powder
- Salt and pepper to taste
- 1/4 cup shredded cheddar cheese (optional)

Mode of Preparation

1. Preheat the oven to 375°F (190°C).
2. Cook quinoa according to package instructions.
3. In a large skillet, cook ground turkey until browned.
4. Add diced tomatoes, black beans, corn, cumin, chili powder, salt, and pepper. Stir in cooked quinoa.
5. Stuff the bell pepper halves with the turkey and quinoa mixture.
6. Bake for 25-30 minutes or until peppers are tender.
7. Optionally, sprinkle shredded cheddar cheese on top during the last 5 minutes of baking.

Nutritional Information (Per Serving)

- **Calories:** Approx. 380

- **Protein:** Approx. 25g
- **Carbohydrates:** Approx. 40g
- **Fiber:** Approx. 8g
- **Total Fat:** Approx. 12g

Serving Size: 2 stuffed bell pepper halves.

Cooking Time: 35 minutes.

Preparation Time: 25 minutes.

16. Vegetarian Quinoa and Black Bean Bow
Health Benefits

- Quinoa and black beans provide plant-based protein and fiber.
- Avocado contributes healthy fats and creamy texture.
- Mixed vegetables add essential vitamins and minerals.

Ingredients

- 1/2 cup quinoa (uncooked)
- 1 cup black beans (canned, drained, and rinsed)

- 1/2 avocado, diced
- 1/4 cup corn kernels
- 1/4 cup red onion, finely chopped
- 1/4 cup cherry tomatoes, halved
- 1/4 cup cilantro, chopped
- Juice of one lime
- 1 tablespoon olive oil
- Salt and pepper to taste

Mode of Preparation

1. Cook quinoa according to package instructions.
2. In a bowl, combine cooked quinoa, black beans, avocado, corn, red onion, cherry tomatoes, cilantro, olive oil, lime juice, salt, and pepper.
3. Toss gently to combine.

Nutritional Information (Per Serving)

- **Calories:** Approx. 350
- **Protein:** Approx. 15g

- **Carbohydrates:** Approx. 45g
- **Fiber:** Approx. 10g
- **Total Fat:** Approx. 15g

Serving Size: 1 bowl.

Cooking Time: 20 minutes.

Preparation Time: 15 minutes.

17. Asian-Inspired Tofu and Vegetable Stir-Fry

Health Benefits

- Tofu provides plant-based protein with minimal saturated fat.
- Assorted vegetables offer vitamins and minerals.
- Soy sauce and ginger add flavor without excess calories.

Ingredients

- 6 oz firm tofu, cubed
- 1/2 cup broccoli florets
- 1/2 cup snap peas

- 1/2 cup carrots, thinly sliced
- 1/4 cup low-sodium soy sauce
- 1 tablespoon sesame oil
- 1 tablespoon ginger, minced
- 2 cloves garlic, minced
- 1 tablespoon olive oil (for cooking)
- Sesame seeds for garnish

Mode of Preparation

1. Olive oil should be heated in a large skillet over medium heat.
2. Add tofu cubes and stir-fry until golden brown.
3. Add broccoli, snap peas, and carrots. Stir-fry until vegetables are tender-crisp.
4. In a small bowl, mix soy sauce, sesame oil, ginger, and garlic. Pour over the tofu and vegetables. Toss to coat.
5. Garnish with sesame seeds.

1300 CALORIE MEAL PLAN FOR WEIGHT LOSS

Nutritional Information (Per Serving)

- **Calories:** Approx. 330
- **Protein:** Approx. 20g
- **Carbohydrates:** Approx. 25g
- **Fiber:** Approx. 8g
- **Total Fat:** Approx. 18g

Serving Size: 1 plate.

Cooking Time: 25 minutes.

Preparation Time: 20 minutes.

18. Mediterranean Quinoa Salad with Chickpeas

Health Benefits

- Quinoa and chickpeas provide a combination of protein and fiber.
- Vegetables and olives offer vitamins and healthy fats.
- Feta cheese adds a savory touch.

Ingredients

- 1/2 cup quinoa (uncooked)

- Canned chickpeas, drained and rinsed of 1 cup
- 1/4 cup cherry tomatoes, halved
- 1/4 cup cucumber, diced
- 1/4 cup red onion, finely chopped
- 2 tablespoons Kalamata olives, sliced
- 2 tablespoons feta cheese, crumbled
- 1 tablespoon olive oil
- Juice of one lemon
- 1 teaspoon dried oregano
- Salt and pepper to taste

Mode of Preparation

1. Cook quinoa according to package instructions.
2. In a bowl, combine cooked quinoa, chickpeas, cherry tomatoes, cucumber, red onion, olives, feta cheese, olive oil, lemon juice, oregano, salt, and pepper.
3. Toss gently to combine.

Nutritional Information (Per Serving)

- **Calories:** Approx. 360
- **Protein:** Approx. 15g
- **Carbohydrates:** Approx. 45g
- **Fiber:** Approx. 10g
- **Total Fat:** Approx. 15g

Serving Size: 1 bowl.

Cooking Time: 20 minutes.

Preparation Time: 15 minutes.

19. Salmon and Asparagus Foil Pack

Health Benefits

- Salmon provides omega-3 fatty acids for heart health.
- Asparagus offers vitamins and antioxidants.
- Cooking in foil helps retain nutrients.

Ingredients

- 2 salmon fillets
- 1/2 lb asparagus spears, trimmed
- 1 tablespoon olive oil
- 1 lemon, sliced
- 2 cloves garlic, minced
- 1 teaspoon dried dill
- Salt and pepper to taste

Mode of Preparation

1. Preheat the oven to 400°F (200°C).
2. Place each salmon fillet on a piece of foil.

3. Arrange asparagus around the salmon.
4. Drizzle olive oil over salmon and asparagus.
5. Sprinkle minced garlic, dried dill, salt, and pepper over each fillet.
6. Place lemon slices on top.
7. Seal the foil packs and bake for 15-20 minutes or until salmon is cooked through.

Nutritional Information (Per Serving)

- **Calories:** Approx. 380
- **Protein:** Approx. 30g
- **Carbohydrates:** Approx. 10g
- **Fiber:** Approx. 4g
- **Total Fat:** Approx. 20g

Serving Size: 1 foil pack.

Cooking Time: 20 minutes.

Preparation Time: 15 minutes.

20. Caprese Wrap with Turkey

Health Benefits

- Turkey provides lean protein with low fat.
- Tomatoes offer antioxidants, vitamins, and minerals.
- Fresh mozzarella adds calcium and a creamy texture.

Ingredients

- 4 oz turkey breast slices
- 1 whole-grain wrap
- 1/2 cup cherry tomatoes, halved
- 1/4 cup fresh mozzarella balls
- Fresh basil leaves
- 1 tablespoon balsamic glaze
- Salt and pepper to taste

Mode of Preparation

1. Warm the whole-grain wrap.
2. Layer turkey slices, cherry tomatoes, fresh mozzarella, and basil leaves on the wrap.

3. Drizzle with balsamic glaze.
4. Season with salt and pepper.
5. Roll the wrap tightly.

Nutritional Information (Per Serving)

- **Calories:** Approx. 350
- **Protein:** Approx. 30g
- **Carbohydrates:** Approx. 30g
- **Fiber:** Approx. 5g
- **Total Fat:** Approx. 15g

Serving Size:

- 1 wrap.

Cooking Time:

- 10 minutes.

Preparation Time:

- 15 minutes.

CHAPTER 3

Dinner Recipes

1. Grilled Salmon with Asparagus

Health Benefits

- Salmon is rich in omega-3 fatty acids for heart health.
- Asparagus provides vitamins A, C, and K.
- Low-calorie, high-protein option for weight loss.

Ingredients (for 2 servings):

- 2 salmon fillets (6 oz each)
- 1 bunch asparagus, trimmed
- 2 tablespoons olive oil
- 1 lemon, sliced
- Salt and pepper to taste

Mode of Preparation

- Preheat the grill.
- Salmon and asparagus should be seasoned with olive oil, salt, and pepper.

- Salmon should be grilled for 4-5 minutes per side, and asparagus for 3-4 minutes.
- Serve with a squeeze of lemon.

Nutritional Information (Per Serving)

- **Calories:** Approx. 350
- **Protein:** Approx. 35g
- **Carbohydrates:** Approx. 10g
- **Fiber:** Approx. 4g
- **Total Fat:** Approx. 20g

Serving Size: 1 grilled salmon fillet with asparagus.

Cooking Time: 10 minutes.

Preparation Time: 15 minutes.

2. Veggie and Chicken Skewers

Health Benefits

- Lean chicken provides high-quality protein.
- Colorful veggies offer a variety of antioxidants.
- Low-calorie and satisfying for weight management.

Ingredients

- 2 boneless, skinless chicken breasts (8 oz each)
- 1 zucchini, sliced
- 1 bell pepper, cut into chunks
- 1 red onion, cut into wedges
- 2 tablespoons olive oil
- 1 teaspoon dried oregano
- Salt and pepper to taste

Mode of Preparation

- Preheat the grill. Cut chicken into cubes.
- Thread chicken, zucchini, bell pepper, and red onion onto skewers.

- Drizzle with olive oil, sprinkle with oregano, salt, and pepper.
- Grill for 12-15 minutes, turning occasionally.

Nutritional Information (Per Serving)

- **Calories:** Approx. 320
- **Protein:** Approx. 30g
- **Carbohydrates:** Approx. 15g
- **Fiber:** Approx. 4g
- **Total Fat:** Approx. 15g

Serving Size: 1 plate of chicken and veggie skewers.

Cooking Time: 15 minutes.

Preparation Time: 20 minutes.

3. Quinoa and Chickpea Buddha Bowl

Health Benefits

- Quinoa provides complete proteins.
- Chickpeas offer fiber and plant-based protein.
- Loaded with veggies for vitamins and minerals.

Ingredients

- 1 cup quinoa, cooked
- 1 can (15 oz) chickpeas, drained and rinsed
- 2 cups mixed greens
- 1 cucumber, diced
- 1 avocado, sliced
- 1/4 cup feta cheese, crumbled
- 2 tablespoons balsamic vinaigrette

Mode of Preparation

- Assemble bowls with quinoa, chickpeas, mixed greens, cucumber, avocado, and feta.
- Drizzle with balsamic vinaigrette.

Nutritional Information (Per Serving)

- **Calories:** Approx. 380
- **Protein:** Approx. 15g
- **Carbohydrates:** Approx. 50g
- **Fiber:** Approx. 12g
- **Total Fat:** Approx. 15g

Serving Size: 1 Buddha bowl.

Cooking Time: 20 minutes.

Preparation Time: 15 minutes.

4. Turkey and Vegetable Stir-Fry

Health Benefits

- Lean turkey is a good source of protein.
- Mixed vegetables provide essential nutrients.
- Stir-frying retains nutrients with minimal added fats.

Ingredients

- 1 lb ground turkey
- 4 cups mixed stir-fry vegetables (broccoli, bell peppers, snap peas)
- 2 tablespoons soy sauce
- 1 tablespoon sesame oil
- 1 tablespoon olive oil
- 2 cloves garlic, minced
- 1 teaspoon ginger, minced

Mode of Preparation

- In a wok or skillet, brown ground turkey in olive oil.
- Add mixed vegetables, garlic, and ginger.
- It should be Stirred in soy sauce and sesame oil, cook until vegetables are tender.

Nutritional Information (Per Serving)

- **Calories:** Approx. 330
- **Protein:** Approx. 25g

- **Carbohydrates:** Approx. 15g
- **Fiber:** Approx. 5g
- **Total Fat:** Approx. 18g

Serving Size: 1 plate of turkey and vegetable stir-fry.

Cooking Time: 15 minutes.

Preparation Time: 20 minutes.

5. Lentil and Vegetable Soup
Health Benefits

- Lentils offer a good source of plant-based protein and fiber.
- Abundance of vegetables provides vitamins and minerals.
- Low-calorie and satisfying for weight loss.

Ingredients

- 1 cup dry lentils
- 1 onion, diced
- 2 carrots, sliced

- 2 celery stalks, diced
- 2 cloves garlic, minced
- 1 can (14 oz) diced tomatoes
- 6 cups vegetable broth
- 1 teaspoon cumin
- 1 teaspoon paprika
- Salt and pepper to taste
- 2 tablespoons olive oil

Mode of Preparation

- Rinse lentils and set aside.
- In a large pot, sauté onion, carrots, celery, and garlic in olive oil until softened.
- Add lentils, diced tomatoes, vegetable broth, cumin, paprika, salt, and pepper. Simmer until lentils are tender.

Nutritional Information (Per Serving)

- **Calories:** Approx. 300
- **Protein:** Approx. 20g
- **Carbohydrates:** Approx. 50g
- **Fiber:** Approx. 15g
- **Total Fat:** Approx. 5g

Serving Size: 1 bowl.

Cooking Time: 30 minutes.

Preparation Time: 20 minutes.

6. Eggplant and Chickpea Curry

Health Benefits

- Chickpeas offer plant-based protein and fiber.
- Eggplant has calories and its high in antioxidants.
- Rich in spices for added flavor without excess calories.

Ingredients

- 1 can (15 oz) chickpeas, drained and rinsed
- 1 large eggplant, diced
- 1 onion, chopped
- 2 tomatoes, diced
- 1 can (14 oz) coconut milk
- 2 tablespoons curry powder
- 1 teaspoon cumin
- 1 teaspoon coriander
- 2 tablespoons olive oil
- Salt and pepper to taste

Mode of Preparation

- Sauté onion in olive oil until translucent. Add eggplant, chickpeas, tomatoes, curry powder, cumin, and coriander.
- Stir in coconut milk and simmer until eggplant is tender.

- Season with salt and pepper.

Nutritional Information (Per Serving)

- **Calories:** Approx. 320
- **Protein:** Approx. 15g
- **Carbohydrates:** Approx. 30g
- **Fiber:** Approx. 12g
- **Total Fat:** Approx. 18g

Serving Size: 1 bowl.

Cooking Time: 25 minutes.

Preparation Time: 15 minutes.

7. Zucchini Noodles with Pesto and Cherry Tomatoes

Health Benefits

- Zucchini noodles are low in calories and high in vitamins.
- Pesto provides healthy fats and flavor.
- Cherry tomatoes add antioxidants and freshness.

Ingredients

- 4 medium zucchinis, spiralized
- 1 cup cherry tomatoes, halved
- 1/2 cup basil pesto
- 1/4 cup grated Parmesan cheese
- 2 tablespoons pine nuts
- Salt and pepper to taste

Mode of Preparation

- Sauté zucchini noodles in a pan until slightly softened.

- Toss with cherry tomatoes, pesto, Parmesan, and pine nuts.
- Season with salt and pepper.

Nutritional Information (Per Serving)

- **Calories:** Approx. 300
- **Protein:** Approx. 10g
- **Carbohydrates:** Approx. 20g
- **Fiber:** Approx. 5g
- **Total Fat:** Approx. 20g

Serving Size: 1 plate.

Cooking Time: 10 minutes.

Preparation Time: 15 minutes.

8. Baked Sweet Potato and Black Bean Quesadillas

Health Benefits

- Sweet potatoes offer fiber and vitamins.
- Black beans provide plant-based protein.
- Baking reduces added fats.

Ingredients

- 2 Big size sweet potatoes, peeled and diced
- Black beans, drained and rinsed of 1 can (15 oz)
- 1 cup corn kernels
- 1 teaspoon cumin
- 1 teaspoon chili powder
- 8 whole-grain tortillas
- 1 cup shredded cheese (cheddar or Mexican blend)
- Salsa and Greek yogurt for serving

Mode of Preparation

- Roast sweet potatoes until tender. Mash them with black beans, corn, cumin, and chili powder.

- Spread the mixture on half of each tortilla, top with cheese, and fold in half.
- Bake until the tortillas are crispy and the cheese is melted.
- Serve with salsa and Greek yogurt.

Nutritional Information (Per Serving)

- **Calories:** Approx. 350
- **Protein:** Approx. 15g
- **Carbohydrates:** Approx. 55g
- **Fiber:** Approx. 12g
- **Total Fat:** Approx. 10g

Serving Size: 1 quesadilla.

Cooking Time: 25 minutes.

Preparation Time: 20 minutes.

9. Spinach and Mushroom Stuffed Chicken Breast

Health Benefits

- Chicken breast offers lean protein.
- Spinach and mushrooms provide vitamins and minerals.
- Baking maintains flavors without excessive fats.

Ingredients

- Chicken without bones and, skinless chicken breasts (6 oz each)
- 2 cups fresh spinach
- 1 cup mushrooms, sliced
- 2 cloves garlic, minced
- 1/4 cup feta cheese, crumbled
- 1 tablespoon olive oil
- Salt and pepper to taste

Mode of Preparation

- Preheat the oven to 375°F (190°C).

- Sauté mushrooms and garlic in olive oil until softened. Add spinach and cook until wilted.
- Cut a pocket into each chicken breast, stuff with the spinach-mushroom mixture, and top with feta.
- Bake until chicken is cooked through.

Nutritional Information

- **Calories:** Approx. 320
- **Protein:** Approx. 35g
- **Carbohydrates:** Approx. 10g
- **Fiber:** Approx. 4g
- **Total Fat:** Approx. 15g

Serving Size: 1 stuffed chicken breast.

Cooking Time: 25 minutes.

Preparation Time: 20 minutes.

10. Broccoli and Tofu Stir-Fry

Health Benefits

- Tofu provides plant-based protein.
- Broccoli contains vitamins, minerals, and fiber.
- Stir-frying retains nutrients with minimal added fats.

Ingredients

- 1 block firm tofu, cubed
- 4 cups broccoli florets
- 1 carrot, sliced
- 1 bell pepper, sliced
- 2 tablespoons soy sauce
- 1 tablespoon sesame oil
- 1 tablespoon hoisin sauce
- 1 tablespoon olive oil
- 2 cloves garlic, minced
- 1 teaspoon ginger, minced

Mode of Preparation

- Press excess water from tofu, then stir-fry until golden brown in olive oil.
- Add broccoli, carrot, bell pepper, garlic, and ginger.
- Mix in soy sauce, sesame oil, and hoisin sauce.
- Stir-fry until vegetables are tender.

Nutritional Information (Per Serving)

- **Calories:** Approx. 330
- **Protein:** Approx. 20g
- **Carbohydrates:** Approx. 25g
- **Fiber:** Approx. 8g
- **Total Fat:** Approx. 18g

Serving Size: 1 plate.

Cooking Time: 15 minutes.

Preparation Time: 20 minutes.

11. Cauliflower Fried Rice with Shrimp

Health Benefits

- Cauliflower rice is a low-calorie alternative to traditional rice.
- Shrimp provides lean protein.
- Packed with veggies for added nutrients.

Ingredients (for 2 servings):

- 1 lb shrimp, peeled and deveined
- 4 cups cauliflower rice
- Mixed vegetables (peas, carrots, corn) of 1 cup
- 2 eggs, beaten
- 2 tablespoons soy sauce
- 1 tablespoon sesame oil
- 2 green onions, sliced
- 1 tablespoon olive oil
- 1 teaspoon ginger, minced

Mode of Preparation

- In a wok or skillet, sauté shrimp in olive oil until pink. Set aside.
- Stir-fry mixed vegetables and ginger until tender.
- Push vegetables to one side, pour beaten eggs into the pan, and scramble.
- Mix in cauliflower rice, cooked shrimp, soy sauce, and sesame oil.
- Top with sliced green onions.

Nutritional Information (Per Serving)

- **Calories:** Approx. 340
- **Protein:** Approx. 30g
- **Carbohydrates:** Approx. 20g
- **Fiber:** Approx. 6g
- **Total Fat:** Approx. 15g

Serving Size: 1 plate.

Cooking Time: 15 minutes.

Preparation Time: 20 minutes.

12. Stuffed Bell Peppers with Turkey and Quinoa

Health Benefits

- Lean ground turkey provides protein.
- Quinoa offers complete proteins and fiber.
- Bell peppers are rich in vitamins.

Ingredients

- 1 lb ground turkey
- 1 cup quinoa, cooked
- Bell peppers (4), should be halved and get the seeds removed
- Black beans, drained and rinsed of 1 can (15 oz)
- 1 cup corn kernels
- 1 cup salsa
- 1 teaspoon cumin
- 1 teaspoon chili powder
- 1 cup shredded cheese (cheddar or Mexican blend)

Mode of Preparation

- Preheat the oven to 375°F (190°C).
- Brown ground turkey, mix in cooked quinoa, black beans, corn, salsa, cumin, and chili powder.
- Stuff bell peppers with the mixture and top with shredded cheese.
- Bake for 25-30 minutes.

Nutritional Information (Per Serving)

- **Calories:** Approx. 350
- **Protein:** Approx. 25g
- **Carbohydrates:** Approx. 30g
- **Fiber:** Approx. 8g
- **Total Fat:** Approx. 15g

Serving Size: 1 stuffed pepper half.

Cooking Time: 30 minutes.

Preparation Time: 20 minutes.

13. Mediterranean Chickpea Salad

Health Benefits

- Chickpeas provide plant-based protein and fiber.
- Loaded with fresh vegetables for vitamins and minerals.
- Olive oil offers healthy fats.

Ingredients

- 1 can (15 oz) chickpeas, drained and rinsed
- 1 cucumber, diced
- 1 cup cherry tomatoes, halved
- 1/2 red onion, finely chopped
- 1/2 cup Kalamata olives, sliced
- 1/4 cup feta cheese, crumbled
- 2 tablespoons extra virgin olive oil
- 1 tablespoon red wine vinegar
- 1 teaspoon dried oregano
- Salt and pepper to taste

Mode of Preparation

- Combine chickpeas, cucumber, cherry tomatoes, red onion, olives, and feta in a large bowl.
- Whisk together olive oil, red wine vinegar, oregano, salt, and pepper in a small bowl.
- The dressing should be drizzled over the salad and toss to combine.

Nutritional Information (Per Serving)

- **Calories:** Approx. 320
- **Protein:** Approx. 15g
- **Carbohydrates:** Approx. 35g
- **Fiber:** Approx. 10g
- **Total Fat:** Approx. 15g

Serving Size: 1 plate.

Preparation Time: 15 minutes.

14. Spaghetti Squash with Turkey Bolognese
Health Benefits

- Spaghetti squash is a low-calorie alternative to pasta.
- Lean ground turkey provides protein.
- Rich in vegetables for added nutrients.

Ingredients

- 1 medium spaghetti squash, halved and seeds removed
- 1 lb ground turkey
- 1 can (14 oz) crushed tomatoes
- 1 onion, diced
- 2 cloves garlic, minced
- 1 teaspoon dried basil
- 1 teaspoon dried oregano
- Salt and pepper to taste
- Fresh basil for garnish

Mode of Preparation

- Preheat the oven to 375°F (190°C). Roast spaghetti squash for 30-40 minutes.

- In a skillet, brown ground turkey. Add onions and garlic, cook until softened.

- Stir in crushed tomatoes, basil, oregano, salt, and pepper. Simmer.

- Scrape the cooked spaghetti squash with a fork to create "noodles."

- Top with turkey bolognese and garnish with fresh basil.

Nutritional Information (Per Serving)

- **Calories:** Approx. 350

- **Protein:** Approx. 30g

- **Carbohydrates:** Approx. 30g

- **Fiber:** Approx. 10g

- **Total Fat:** Approx. 15g

Serving Size: 1 plate.

Cooking Time: 40 minutes.

Preparation Time: 20 minutes.

15. Grilled Veggie and Hummus Wrap

Health Benefits

- Grilled vegetables provide vitamins and minerals.
- Hummus adds plant-based protein and healthy fats.
- Whole-grain wrap for additional fiber.

Ingredients

- 2 whole-grain wraps
- 1 zucchini, sliced
- 1 bell pepper, sliced
- 1 eggplant, sliced
- 1 cup cherry tomatoes, halved
- 1/2 cup hummus
- 1 tablespoon olive oil

- 1 teaspoon dried thyme
- Salt and pepper to taste

Mode of Preparation

- Preheat the grill. Toss zucchini, bell pepper, eggplant, and cherry tomatoes in olive oil, thyme, salt, and pepper.
- Grill until vegetables are tender.
- Spread hummus on each wrap, add grilled veggies, and roll up.

Nutritional Information (Per Serving)

- **Calories:** Approx. 330
- **Protein:** Approx. 12g
- **Carbohydrates:** Approx. 45g
- **Fiber:** Approx. 10g
- **Total Fat:** Approx. 15g

Serving Size: 1 wrap.

Cooking Time: 15 minutes.

Preparation Time: 20 minutes.

16. Baked Chicken with Lemon and Rosemary

Health Benefits

- Chicken breast provides lean source of protein.
- Lemon adds freshness and vitamin C.
- Rosemary provides antioxidants.

Ingredients (for 2 servings):

- Boneless, skinless chicken breasts of 2 Pcs
- 1 lemon, sliced
- 2 tablespoons olive oil
- 2 teaspoons dried rosemary
- Salt and pepper to taste

Mode of Preparation

- Preheat the oven to 375°F (190°C).
- Chicken breast should be placed in a baking dish.
- It should be drizzled with olive oil, sprinkle with rosemary, salt, and pepper.
- Top with lemon slices.

- It should be baked for 25-30 minutes or until chicken is cooked through.

Nutritional Information (Per Serving)

- **Calories:** Approx. 320
- **Protein:** Approx. 35g
- **Carbohydrates:** Approx. 5g
- **Fiber:** Approx. 2g
- **Total Fat:** Approx. 15g

Serving Size: 1 baked chicken breast.

Cooking Time: 30 minutes.

Preparation Time: 15 minutes.

17. Chickpea and Spinach Stuffed Sweet Potatoes
Health Benefits

- Sweet potatoes offer vitamins and fiber.
- Chickpeas provide plant-based protein and fiber.
- Spinach adds essential nutrients.

Ingredients

- 2 medium sweet potatoes
- 1 can (15 oz) chickpeas, drained and rinsed
- 2 cups fresh spinach
- 1 red onion, finely chopped
- 2 cloves garlic, minced
- 2 tablespoons olive oil
- 1 teaspoon cumin
- 1 teaspoon paprika
- Salt and pepper to taste
- Greek yogurt for serving

Mode of Preparation

- Preheat the oven to 400°F (200°C). Prick sweet potatoes with a fork and bake for 45-50 minutes.
- In a skillet, sauté red onion and garlic in olive oil.
- Chickpeas, spinach, cumin, paprika, salt, and pepper should be added.

- Cut sweet potatoes in half, fluff the insides with a fork, and stuff with the chickpea-spinach mixture.
- It should be dished with a dollop of Greek yogurt.

Nutritional Information (Per Serving)

- **Calories:** Approx. 340
- **Protein:** Approx. 15g
- **Carbohydrates:** Approx. 55g
- **Fiber:** Approx. 10g
- **Total Fat:** Approx. 10g

Serving Size: 1 stuffed sweet potato.

Cooking Time: 50 minutes.

Preparation Time: 20 minutes.

18. Teriyaki Salmon with Broccoli and Quinoa

Health Benefits

- Salmon gives omega-3 fatty acids and protein.
- Broccoli is rich in vitamins and fiber.
- Quinoa offers complete proteins.

Ingredients

- 2 salmon fillets (6 oz each)
- 1 cup quinoa, cooked
- 2 cups broccoli florets
- 1/4 cup low-sodium teriyaki sauce
- 1 tablespoon olive oil
- Sesame seeds for garnish

Mode of Preparation

- Preheat the oven to 400°F (200°C).
- Place salmon on a baking sheet. Brush with teriyaki sauce and bake for 15-18 minutes or until cooked through.

- Steam or roast broccoli until tender.
- Serve salmon over a bed of quinoa with a side of broccoli. Garnish with sesame seeds.

Nutritional Information (Per Serving)

- **Calories:** Approx. 380
- **Protein:** Approx. 30g
- **Carbohydrates:** Approx. 40g
- **Fiber:** Approx. 6g
- **Total Fat:** Approx. 15g

Serving Size: 1 plate.

Cooking Time: 18 minutes.

Preparation Time: 20 minutes.

19. Blackened Shrimp Tacos with Avocado Lime Crema

Health Benefits

- Shrimp is low in calorie
- Avocado offers healthy fats.
- Whole-grain tortillas add fiber.

Ingredients

- 1 lb shrimp, peeled and deveined
- 1 tablespoon blackening seasoning
- 1 tablespoon olive oil
- 4 whole-grain tortillas
- 1 cup shredded cabbage
- 1/2 cup cherry tomatoes, halved
- 1/4 cup red onion, finely chopped
- 1/2 avocado, sliced

Mode of Preparation

- Toss shrimp in blackening seasoning.

- In a skillet, heat olive oil and cook shrimp until opaque.
- Assemble tacos with shredded cabbage, cherry tomatoes, red onion, and avocado slices.

Nutritional Information (Per Serving)

- **Calories:** Approx. 340
- **Protein:** Approx. 25g
- **Carbohydrates:** Approx. 30g
- **Fiber:** Approx. 8g
- **Total Fat:** Approx. 15g

Serving Size: 2 tacos.

Cooking Time: 10 minutes.

Preparation Time: 15 minutes.

20. Quinoa and Black Bean Stuffed Bell Peppers
Health Benefits

- Quinoa provides complete proteins and fiber.
- Black beans offer plant-based protein.
- Bell peppers are rich in vitamins.

Ingredients (for 2 servings):

- Bell peppers (4), should be halved and get the seeds removed
- 1 cup quinoa, cooked
- Black beans, drained and rinsed of 1 can (15 oz)
- 1 cup corn kernels
- 1 cup salsa
- 1 teaspoon cumin
- 1 teaspoon chili powder
- 1 cup shredded cheese (cheddar or Mexican blend)

Mode of Preparation

- Preheat the oven to 375°F (190°C).

- In a bowl, mix cooked quinoa, black beans, corn, salsa, cumin, and chili powder.
- Stuff bell peppers with the quinoa mixture and top with shredded cheese.
- Bake for 25-30 minutes.

Nutritional Information (Per Serving)

- **Calories:** Approx. 350
- **Protein:** Approx. 20g
- **Carbohydrates:** Approx. 55g
- **Fiber:** Approx. 12g
- **Total Fat:** Approx. 10g

Serving Size: 1 stuffed pepper half.

Cooking Time: 30 minutes.

Preparation Time: 20 minutes.

CHAPTER 4

Side dishes recipes

1. Roasted Brussels Sprouts with Balsamic Glaze

Health Benefits

- Brussels sprouts are rich in fiber, aiding digestion.
- Balsamic vinegar provides antioxidants and adds flavor without excess calories.
- Low-calorie option supporting weight loss.

Ingredients

- 1 lb Brussels sprouts, halved
- 2 tablespoons olive oil
- 2 tablespoons balsamic vinegar
- Salt and pepper to taste

Mode of Preparation

- Toss Brussels sprouts in olive oil, balsamic vinegar, salt, and pepper.

- Roast in the oven at 400°F (200°C) for 20-25 minutes until golden brown.

Nutritional Information (Per Serving)

- **Calories:** Approx. 90
- **Protein:** Approx. 4g
- **Carbohydrates:** Approx. 10g
- **Fiber:** Approx. 4g
- **Total Fat:** Approx. 5g

Serving Size: 1/2 cup.

Cooking Time: 25 minutes.

Preparation Time: 10 minutes.

2. Quinoa and Vegetable Stir-Fry
Health Benefits

- Quinoa offers complete proteins and essential amino acids.
- Assorted vegetables provide vitamins and minerals.
- Low-calorie, high-fiber option for weight management.

Ingredients

- 1 cup quinoa, cooked
- Mixed vegetables (bell peppers, broccoli, carrots) of 2 cups
- 2 tablespoons soy sauce
- 1 tablespoon sesame oil
- 1 tablespoon olive oil
- 2 cloves garlic, minced
- 1 teaspoon ginger, minced

Mode of Preparation

- In a pan, heat olive oil, sauté garlic, and ginger.
- Add mixed vegetables and stir-fry until tender.
- Mix in cooked quinoa, soy sauce, and sesame oil.

Nutritional Information (Per Serving)

- **Calories:** Approx. 180
- **Protein:** Approx. 6g
- **Carbohydrates:** Approx. 30g
- **Fiber:** Approx. 5g
- **Total Fat:** Approx. 5g

Serving Size: 1 cup.

Cooking Time: 15 minutes.

Preparation Time: 15 minutes.

3. Cucumber and Tomato Salad with Feta

Health Benefits

- Cucumbers are low in calories.
- Tomatoes provide vitamins and antioxidants.
- Feta cheese adds flavor with moderate calorie content.

Ingredients

- 2 large cucumbers, sliced
- 2 cups cherry tomatoes, halved
- 1/2 cup feta cheese, crumbled
- 2 tablespoons olive oil
- 1 tablespoon red wine vinegar
- Fresh basil leaves for garnish
- Salt and pepper to taste

Mode of Preparation

- Combine cucumbers, cherry tomatoes, and feta cheese in a bowl.

- Drizzle with olive oil and red wine vinegar.
- Season with salt and pepper, garnish with fresh basil leaves.

Nutritional Information (Per Serving)

- **Calories:** Approx. 120
- **Protein:** Approx. 5g
- **Carbohydrates:** Approx. 10g
- **Fiber:** Approx. 2g
- **Total Fat:** Approx. 8g

Serving Size: 1 cup.

Preparation Time: 10 minutes.

4. Sauteed Garlic Spinach
Health Benefits

- Spinach is a nutrient-dense leafy green with vitamins and iron.
- Garlic has immune-boosting properties.
- Low-calorie, high-fiber side dish.

Ingredients

- 1 lb fresh spinach leaves
- 2 tablespoons olive oil
- 4 cloves garlic, minced
- Salt and pepper to taste
- Lemon wedges for serving

Mode of Preparation

- In a pan, heat olive oil, sauté minced garlic until fragrant.
- Fresh spinach should be added and toss until wilted.
- Add salt and pepper.

- It should be served with lemon wedges.

Nutritional Information (Per Serving)

- **Calories:** Approx. 70
- **Protein:** Approx. 4g
- **Carbohydrates:** Approx. 5g
- **Fiber:** Approx. 3g
- **Total Fat:** Approx. 5g

Serving Size: 1 cup.

Cooking Time: 5 minutes.

Preparation Time: 5 minutes.

5. Baked Sweet Potato Wedges
Health Benefits

- Sweet potatoes are rich in fiber, vitamins, and antioxidants.
- Baking maintains nutrients without added fats.
- Provides a satisfying and low-calorie alternative to regular fries.

Ingredients

- Cleaned and sliced 4 medium sweet potatoes into wedges.
- 2 tablespoons olive oil
- 1 teaspoon smoked paprika
- 1 teaspoon garlic powder
- Salt and pepper to taste

Mode of Preparation

- Preheat the oven to 400°F (200°C).
- In a bowl, toss sweet potato wedges with olive oil, smoked paprika, garlic powder, salt, and pepper.
- Spread on a baking sheet and bake for 25-30 minutes until golden and crispy.

Nutritional Information (Per Serving)

- **Calories:** Approx. 150
- **Protein:** Approx. 2g
- **Carbohydrates:** Approx. 25g
- **Fiber:** Approx. 4g
- **Total Fat:** Approx. 5g

Serving Size: 1 cup.

Cooking Time: 30 minutes.

Preparation Time: 10 minutes.

6. Greek Salad with Chickpeas

Health Benefits

- Chickpeas add plant-based protein and fiber.
- Colorful vegetables provide antioxidants and vitamins.
- Feta cheese adds a burst of flavor with moderate calorie content.

Ingredients

- 2 cups cherry tomatoes, halved
- 1 cucumber, diced
- 1 cup Kalamata olives, pitted
- 1 can (15 oz) chickpeas, drained and rinsed
- 1/2 cup feta cheese, crumbled
- 2 tablespoons olive oil
- 1 tablespoon red wine vinegar
- 1 teaspoon dried oregano
- Salt and pepper to taste

Mode of Preparation

- In a large bowl, combine cherry tomatoes, cucumber, olives, chickpeas, and feta cheese.
- Drizzle with olive oil and red wine vinegar.
- Sprinkle with dried oregano, season with salt and pepper. Toss gently.

Nutritional Information (Per Serving)

- **Calories:** Approx. 180
- **Protein:** Approx. 6g
- **Carbohydrates:** Approx. 20g
- **Fiber:** Approx. 6g
- **Total Fat:** Approx. 10g

Serving Size: 1 cup.

Preparation Time: 15 minutes.

7. Cauliflower Rice Pilaf

Health Benefits

- Cauliflower rice is a low-calorie alternative to traditional rice.
- Mixed vegetables provide vitamins and minerals.
- Light and flavorful side dish.

Ingredients

- Cauliflower of 1 head, grated into rice-like texture
- Mixed vegetables (peas, carrots, corn) of 1 cup
- 1/2 cup onion, finely chopped
- 2 tablespoons olive oil
- 1 teaspoon cumin
- 1 teaspoon turmeric
- Salt and pepper to taste
- Fresh cilantro for garnish

Mode of Preparation

- In a pan, sauté chopped onion in olive oil until translucent.
- Add cauliflower rice and mixed vegetables, stir-fry until tender.
- It should be seasoned with cumin, turmeric, salt, and pepper.
- Garnish with fresh cilantro before serving.

Nutritional Information (Per Serving)

- **Calories:** Approx. 100
- **Protein:** Approx. 3g
- **Carbohydrates:** Approx. 10g
- **Fiber:** Approx. 5g
- **Total Fat:** Approx. 6g

Serving Size: 1 cup.

Cooking Time: 15 minutes.

Preparation Time: 10 minutes.

8. Steamed Asparagus with Lemon Garlic Sauce

Health Benefits

- Asparagus is high in fiber and low in calories.
- Lemon garlic sauce adds flavor without excessive calories.
- Quick and easy side dish.

Ingredients

- 1 lb asparagus, trimmed
- 2 tablespoons olive oil
- 2 cloves garlic, minced
- Zest of 1 lemon
- Juice of 1 lemon
- Salt and pepper to taste

Mode of Preparation

- Steam asparagus until tender-crisp.
- Sauté minced garlic in olive oil until fragrant in a pan.

- Lemon zest and juice should be added.
- It should be garnished with salt and pepper.
- Toss steamed asparagus in the lemon garlic sauce.

Nutritional Information (Per Serving)

- **Calories:** Approx. 70
- **Protein:** Approx. 2g
- **Carbohydrates:** Approx. 5g
- **Fiber:** Approx. 3g
- **Total Fat:** Approx. 5g

Serving Size: 1 cup.

Cooking Time: 10 minutes.

Preparation Time: 10 minutes.

9. Mushroom and Spinach Quiche Cups

Health Benefits

- Mushrooms provide a savory, low-calorie option.
- Spinach adds vitamins and minerals.
- High-protein dish for satiety.

Ingredients

- 2 cups mushrooms, chopped
- 2 cups fresh spinach, chopped
- 1/2 cup red bell pepper, diced
- 4 eggs
- 1/2 cup milk (or a dairy-free alternative)
- 1/2 cup feta cheese, crumbled
- Salt and pepper to taste
- Cooking spray

Mode of Preparation

- Preheat the oven to 375°F (190°C).
- In a skillet, sauté mushrooms, spinach, and red bell pepper until cooked.
- In a bowl, whisk together eggs, milk, feta cheese, salt, and pepper.
- Grease muffin cups with cooking spray and distribute the vegetable mixture evenly.
- Egg mixture should be poured over the vegetables.
- It should be baked for 20-25 minutes or until the quiche cups are set.

Nutritional Information (Per Serving)

- **Calories:** Approx. 180
- **Protein:** Approx. 10g
- **Carbohydrates:** Approx. 6g
- **Fiber:** Approx. 2g
- **Total Fat:** Approx. 13g

Serving Size: 2 quiche cups.

Cooking Time: 25 minutes.

Preparation Time: 15 minutes.

10. Spaghetti Squash Primavera
Health Benefits

- Spaghetti squash is a low-calorie, gluten-free alternative to pasta.
- Assorted vegetables provide vitamins and fiber.
- Light and satisfying side dish.

Ingredients

- 1 medium spaghetti squash
- 2 tablespoons olive oil
- 1 cup cherry tomatoes, halved
- 1 cup broccoli florets
- 1 cup bell peppers, sliced
- 2 cloves garlic, minced
- 1 teaspoon Italian seasoning

- Salt and pepper to taste
- Fresh basil for garnish

Mode of Preparation

- Preheat the oven to 375°F (190°C).
- Cut the spaghetti squash in half, remove seeds, and bake cut side down for 30-40 minutes or until tender.
- In a skillet, sauté garlic in olive oil, then add cherry tomatoes, broccoli, and bell peppers.
- Scrape the spaghetti squash with a fork to create "noodles" and add to the skillet.
- Season with Italian seasoning, salt, and pepper. Toss until well combined.
- Garnish with fresh basil before serving.

Nutritional Information (Per Serving)

- **Calories:** Approx. 120
- **Protein:** Approx. 2g
- **Carbohydrates:** Approx. 15g

- **Fiber:** Approx. 4g
- **Total Fat:** Approx. 7g

Serving Size:

- 1 cup.

Cooking Time:

- 40 minutes.

Preparation Time:

- 15 minutes.

11. Baked Zucchini Fries
Health Benefits

- Zucchini is high in water content and also low in calories.
- Baking instead of frying reduces overall calorie intake.
- A flavorful alternative to traditional fries.

Ingredients

- 4 medium zucchini, cut into fries

- 1 cup whole wheat breadcrumbs
- 1/2 cup grated Parmesan cheese
- 2 teaspoons Italian seasoning
- 2 eggs, beaten
- Salt and pepper to taste
- Cooking spray

Mode of Preparation

- Preheat the oven to 425°F (220°C).
- In a bowl, combine breadcrumbs, Parmesan cheese, and Italian seasoning.
- Dip zucchini fries into beaten eggs, then coat with the breadcrumb mixture.
- Place on a baking sheet lined with parchment paper, spray with cooking spray, and bake for 20-25 minutes or until golden brown.

Nutritional Information (Per Serving)

- **Calories:** Approx. 130

- **Protein:** Approx. 7g
- **Carbohydrates:** Approx. 15g
- **Fiber:** Approx. 4g
- **Total Fat:** Approx. 5g

Serving Size: 1 cup.

Cooking Time: 25 minutes.

Preparation Time: 15 minutes.

12. Cabbage and Carrot Slaw
Health Benefits

- Carrots add natural sweetness and beta-carotene.
- A refreshing and crunchy side dish.

Ingredients

- 1/2 small cabbage, shredded
- 2 large carrots, grated
- 1/4 cup plain Greek yogurt
- 2 tablespoons apple cider vinegar

- 1 tablespoon Dijon mustard
- 1 tablespoon honey
- Salt and pepper to taste
- Fresh parsley for garnish

Mode of Preparation

- In a large bowl, combine shredded cabbage and grated carrots.
- In a separate bowl, whisk together Greek yogurt, apple cider vinegar, Dijon mustard, honey, salt, and pepper.
- Pour the dressing over the cabbage and carrots, toss until well coated.
- Garnish with fresh parsley before serving.

Nutritional Information (Per Serving)

- **Calories:** Approx. 70
- **Protein:** Approx. 3g
- **Carbohydrates:** Approx. 15g

- **Fiber:** Approx. 4g
- **Total Fat:** Approx. 1g

Serving Size: 1 cup.

Preparation Time: 15 minutes.

13. Eggplant and Tomato Bake
Health Benefits

- Eggplant is high in fiber and low in calories.
- Tomatoes provide antioxidants, including lycopene.
- Baking retains flavors without added fats.

Ingredients

- 1 large eggplant, sliced
- 2 large tomatoes, sliced
- 1/2 cup mozzarella cheese, shredded
- 2 tablespoons olive oil
- 2 cloves garlic, minced
- 1 teaspoon dried oregano

- Salt and pepper to taste
- Fresh basil for garnish

Mode of Preparation

- Preheat the oven to 375°F (190°C).
- In a baking dish, layer sliced eggplant and tomatoes.
- Drizzle with olive oil, sprinkle minced garlic, dried oregano, salt, and pepper.
- Top with shredded mozzarella.
- It should be baked for 25-30 minutes or until the vegetables are tender.
- Garnish with fresh basil before serving.

Nutritional Information (Per Serving)

- **Calories:** Approx. 120
- **Protein:** Approx. 5g
- **Carbohydrates:** Approx. 15g
- **Fiber:** Approx. 7g
- **Total Fat:** Approx. 6g

Serving Size: 1 cup.

Cooking Time: 30 minutes.

Preparation Time: 15 minutes.

14. Mango Avocado Salsa

Health Benefits

- Mangoes provide natural sweetness and vitamins.
- Avocado adds healthy fats and creaminess.
- A colorful and refreshing topping.

Ingredients

- 1 ripe mango, diced
- 1 avocado, diced
- 1/2 red onion, finely chopped
- 1/4 cup cilantro, chopped
- Juice of 1 lime
- Salt and pepper to taste
- Optional: Jalapeño for spice

Mode of Preparation

- In a bowl, combine diced mango, avocado, red onion, and cilantro.
- Squeeze lime juice over the mixture.
- Season with salt and pepper, and add diced jalapeño if desired.
- Toss gently and refrigerate for at least 30 minutes before serving.

Nutritional Information (Per Serving)

- **Calories:** Approx. 90
- **Protein:** Approx. 1g
- **Carbohydrates:** Approx. 15g
- **Fiber:** Approx. 4g
- **Total Fat:** Approx. 5g

Serving Size: 1/2 cup.

Preparation Time: 15 minutes.

15. Cucumber Avocado Gazpacho

Health Benefits

- Cucumbers are low in calories.
- Avocado adds creaminess and healthy fats.
- Gazpacho is a refreshing, low-calorie soup.

Ingredients

- 2 large cucumbers, peeled and diced
- 1 ripe avocado, diced
- 2 medium tomatoes, diced
- 1/2 red onion, finely chopped
- 1 clove garlic, minced
- 3 cups vegetable broth
- 2 tablespoons olive oil
- 2 tablespoons red wine vinegar
- Salt and pepper to taste
- Fresh basil for garnish

Mode of Preparation

- In a blender, combine cucumbers, avocado, tomatoes, red onion, and garlic.
- Add vegetable broth, olive oil, and red wine vinegar.
- Blend until smooth.
- Season with salt and pepper, then refrigerate for at least 1 hour.
- Garnish with fresh basil before serving.

Nutritional Information (Per Serving)

- **Calories:** Approx. 120
- **Protein:** Approx. 3g
- **Carbohydrates:** Approx. 10g
- **Fiber:** Approx. 4g
- **Total Fat:** Approx. 8g

Serving Size: 1 cup.

Preparation Time: 15 minutes.

Chilling Time: 1 hour.

16. Brussels Sprouts and Apple Salad

Health Benefits

- Brussels sprouts are rich in fiber and vitamins.
- Apples add natural sweetness and additional fiber.
- A crunchy and nutritious salad.

Ingredients

- 1 lb Brussels sprouts, shredded
- 2 apples, thinly sliced
- 1/2 cup walnuts, chopped
- 1/4 cup Parmesan cheese, grated
- 3 tablespoons olive oil
- 2 tablespoons balsamic vinegar
- 1 tablespoon honey
- Salt and pepper to taste

Mode of Preparation

- In a large bowl, combine shredded Brussels sprouts, sliced apples, walnuts, and Parmesan cheese.

- Olive oil, balsamic vinegar, honey, salt, and pepper should be whisked together in a small bowl.
- The dressing should be poured over the salad and toss until well coated.

Nutritional Information (Per Serving)

- **Calories:** Approx. 180
- **Protein:** Approx. 5g
- **Carbohydrates:** Approx. 20g
- **Fiber:** Approx. 6g
- **Total Fat:** Approx. 10g

Serving Size: 1 cup.

Preparation Time: 20 minutes.

17. Quinoa Stuffed Bell Peppers

Health Benefits

- Quinoa provides complete protein and essential amino acids.
- Bell peppers are good source of antioxidants and vitamins.
- A satisfying and nutritious side dish.

Ingredients

- Bell peppers (4), should be halved and get the seeds removed
- 1 cup quinoa, cooked
- Black beans, drained and rinsed of 1 can (15 oz)
- Corn kernels (fresh or frozen) of 1 cup
- 1 cup cherry tomatoes, diced
- 1/2 cup red onion, finely chopped
- 1/4 cup fresh cilantro, chopped
- 1 teaspoon cumin

- 1 teaspoon chili powder
- Salt and pepper to taste
- Juice of 1 lime

Mode of Preparation

- Preheat the oven to 375°F (190°C).
- In a bowl, combine cooked quinoa, black beans, corn, cherry tomatoes, red onion, cilantro, cumin, chili powder, salt, pepper, and lime juice.
- Each bell pepper half should be Stuffed with the quinoa mixture.
- Place in a baking dish and bake for 25-30 minutes or until peppers are tender.

Nutritional Information (Per Serving)

- **Calories:** Approx. 220
- **Protein:** Approx. 9g
- **Carbohydrates:** Approx. 40g
- **Fiber:** Approx. 9g
- **Total Fat:** Approx. 3g

Serving Size: 2 stuffed pepper halves.

Cooking Time: 30 minutes.

Preparation Time: 20 minutes.

18. Mediterranean Quinoa Salad

Health Benefits

- Quinoa offers plant-based protein and essential nutrients.
- Mediterranean flavors with olives and feta for added taste.
- A light and refreshing salad.

Ingredients

- 1 cup quinoa, cooked
- 1 cucumber, diced
- 1 cup cherry tomatoes, halved
- Kalamata olives, pitted and sliced of 1/2 cup
- 1/2 cup feta cheese, crumbled
- 1/4 cup red onion, finely chopped
- 2 tablespoons extra-virgin olive oil
- 1 tablespoon red wine vinegar
- 1 teaspoon dried oregano

- Salt and pepper to taste
- Fresh parsley for garnish

Mode of Preparation

- In a large bowl, combine cooked quinoa, cucumber, cherry tomatoes, olives, feta cheese, and red onion.
- In a small bowl, whisk together olive oil, red wine vinegar, dried oregano, salt, and pepper.
- Dressing should be poured over the salad and toss until well combined.
- Garnish with fresh parsley before serving.

Nutritional Information (Per Serving)

- **Calories:** Approx. 240
- **Protein:** Approx. 9g
- **Carbohydrates:** Approx. 25g
- **Fiber:** Approx. 4g
- **Total Fat:** Approx. 12g

Serving Size: 1 cup.

Preparation Time: 15 minutes.

CHAPTER 5

Snacks Recipes

1. Greek Yogurt Parfait with Berries
Health Benefits

- Greek yogurt provides protein and probiotics for gut health.
- Berries are rich in vitamins, fiber and antioxidants.
- A satisfying and low-calorie snack.

Ingredients

- 1 cup Greek yogurt
- Mixed berries (strawberries, blueberries, raspberries) of 1/2 cup
- 1 tablespoon honey
- 1 tablespoon granola

Mode of Preparation

- Greek yogurt, mixed berries, and granola should be layered in a bowl.

- Drizzle honey on top.
- Repeat the layers if desired.

Nutritional Information (Per Serving)

- **Calories:** Approx. 200
- **Protein:** Approx. 15g
- **Carbohydrates:** Approx. 30g
- **Fiber:** Approx. 5g
- **Total Fat:** Approx. 5g

Serving Size: 1 parfait.

Preparation Time: 5 minutes.

2. Almond Butter and Banana Rice Cakes
Health Benefits

- Almond butter offers healthy fats and protein.
- Bananas provide potassium and natural sweetness.
- Rice cakes are a low-calorie, gluten-free option.

Ingredients

- 2 rice cakes
- 4 tablespoons almond butter
- 2 bananas, sliced

Mode of Preparation

- Almond butter should be spread evenly on each rice cake.
- Top with banana slices.

Nutritional Information (Per Serving)

- **Calories:** Approx. 250
- **Protein:** Approx. 7g
- **Carbohydrates:** Approx. 30g
- **Fiber:** Approx. 5g
- **Total Fat:** Approx. 12g

Serving Size: 1 rice cake.

Preparation Time: 5 minutes.

3. Veggie Sticks with Hummus

Health Benefits

- Hummus provides plant-based protein and healthy fats.
- Colorful veggies offer vitamins and fiber.
- A crunchy and satisfying snack.

Ingredients

- 1 cup hummus
- 2 carrots, sliced
- 2 cucumbers, sliced
- 1 bell pepper, sliced

Mode of Preparation

- Arrange veggie sticks on a plate.
- Dish with a side of hummus for dipping.

Nutritional Information (Per Serving)

- **Calories:** Approx. 180
- **Protein:** Approx. 7g

- **Carbohydrates:** Approx. 20g
- **Fiber:** Approx. 7g
- **Total Fat:** Approx. 9g

Serving Size: 1 plate of veggie sticks with hummus.

Preparation Time: 10 minutes.

4. Cottage Cheese and Pineapple Cups
Health Benefits

- Cottage cheese provide protein and calcium.
- Pineapple is good as natural sweetness and its also vitamin C.
- A refreshing and protein-packed snack.

Ingredients

- 1 cup low-fat cottage cheese
- 1 cup fresh pineapple, diced

Mode of Preparation

- In individual cups, layer cottage cheese and diced pineapple.

Nutritional Information (Per Serving)

- **Calories:** Approx. 180
- **Protein:** Approx. 20g
- **Carbohydrates:** Approx. 20g
- **Fiber:** Approx. 2g
- **Total Fat:** Approx. 3g

Serving Size: 1 cup.

Preparation Time: 5 minutes.

5. Whole Grain Crackers with Avocado
Health Benefits

- Avocado provides healthy fats and vitamins.
- Whole grain crackers offer fiber and complex carbohydrates.
- A satisfying and heart-healthy snack.

Ingredients

- 8 whole grain crackers
- 1 large avocado, mashed

- Salt and pepper to taste

Mode of Preparation

- Spread mashed avocado on each whole grain cracker.
- Season with salt and pepper.

Nutritional Information (Per Serving)

- **Calories:** Approx. 250
- **Protein:** Approx. 5g
- **Carbohydrates:** Approx. 30g
- **Fiber:** Approx. 7g
- **Total Fat:** Approx. 14g

Serving Size: 4 crackers with avocado.

Preparation Time: 5 minutes.

6. Berry and Nut Smoothie Bowl
Health Benefits

- Berries offer antioxidants and vitamins.
- Nuts provide healthy fats and protein.
- A nutrient-dense and refreshing snack.

Ingredients

- Mixed berries (strawberries, blueberries, raspberries) of 1/2 cup
- 1/2 banana, frozen
- 1/2 cup low-fat Greek yogurt
- 1 tablespoon chia seeds
- 1 tablespoon almond butter
- 1/4 cup granola

Mode of Preparation

- Blend mixed berries, frozen banana, Greek yogurt, and almond butter until smooth.
- Pour into a bowl and top with chia seeds and granola.

Nutritional Information (Per Serving)

- **Calories:** Approx. 300
- **Protein:** Approx. 15g
- **Carbohydrates:** Approx. 40g
- **Fiber:** Approx. 8g
- **Total Fat:** Approx. 12g

Serving Size: 1 smoothie bowl.

Preparation Time: 10 minutes.

7. Roasted Chickpeas Snack
Health Benefits

- Chickpeas are rich in protein and fiber.
- Olive oil provides healthy fats.

Ingredients

- Chickpeas, drained and rinsed of 2 cans (15 oz each)
- 2 tablespoons olive oil
- 1 teaspoon smoked paprika
- 1/2 teaspoon cumin
- 1/2 teaspoon garlic powder
- Salt and pepper to taste

Mode of Preparation

- Preheat the oven to 400°F (200°C).
- In a bowl, toss chickpeas with olive oil, smoked paprika, cumin, garlic powder, salt, and pepper.
- Spread the chickpeas on a baking sheet and roast for 25-30 minutes, or until crispy.

Nutritional Information (Per Serving)

- **Calories:** Approx. 200
- **Protein:** Approx. 10g
- **Carbohydrates:** Approx. 25g

- **Fiber:** Approx. 7g
- **Total Fat:** Approx. 8g

Serving Size: 1/2 cup.

Preparation Time: 35 minutes.

8. Cucumber Avocado Salsa
Health Benefits

- Avocado provides healthy fats and creamy texture.
- Cucumbers provide hydration and vitamins.
- A light and flavorful snack.

Ingredients

- 1 large cucumber, diced
- 1 avocado, diced
- 1/2 cup cherry tomatoes, halved
- 1/4 cup red onion, finely chopped
- 1/4 cup fresh cilantro, chopped
- Juice of 1 lime

- Salt and pepper to taste

Mode of Preparation

- In a bowl, combine diced cucumber, avocado, cherry tomatoes, red onion, and cilantro.

- It should be Drizzled with lime juice and season with salt and pepper.

- Mix well.

Nutritional Information (Per Serving)

- **Calories:** Approx. 150

- **Protein:** Approx. 3g

- **Carbohydrates:** Approx. 15g

- **Fiber:** Approx. 7g

- **Total Fat:** Approx. 10g

Serving Size: 1 cup.

Preparation Time: 15 minutes.

9. Edamame and Sea Salt Snack

Health Benefits

- Edamame provides plant-based protein and fiber.
- Sea salt adds flavor without excess calories.
- A crunchy and satisfying snack.

Ingredients

- 2 cups frozen edamame, thawed
- 1 tablespoon olive oil
- Sea salt to taste

Mode of Preparation

- In a bowl, toss edamame with olive oil until evenly coated.
- Spread the edamame on a baking sheet.
- Roast in the oven at 375°F (190°C) for 15-20 minutes or until crispy.
- Sprinkle with sea salt and toss before serving.

Nutritional Information (Per Serving)

- **Calories:** Approx. 150
- **Protein:** Approx. 12g
- **Carbohydrates:** Approx. 10g
- **Fiber:** Approx. 6g
- **Total Fat:** Approx. 8g

Serving Size: 1 cup.

Preparation Time: 25 minutes.

10. Dark Chocolate and Almond Trail Mix

Health Benefits

- Almonds provide healthy fats and protein.
- Dark chocolate gives antioxidants and a touch of sweetness.
- A satisfying and indulgent snack.

Ingredients

- 1/2 cup almonds, unsalted
- 1/4 cup dark chocolate chips

- 1/4 cup dried cranberries
- 1/4 cup pumpkin seeds
- 1/4 cup coconut flakes

Mode of Preparation

- In a bowl, combine almonds, dark chocolate chips, dried cranberries, pumpkin seeds, and coconut flakes.
- Mix well and divide into individual servings.

Nutritional Information (Per Serving)

- **Calories:** Approx. 250
- **Protein:** Approx. 6g
- **Carbohydrates:** Approx. 20g
- **Fiber:** Approx. 5g
- **Total Fat:** Approx. 16g

Serving Size: 1/2 cup.

Preparation Time: 10 minutes.

11. Crispy Kale Chips

Health Benefits

- Kale supplies vitamins A, K, and C.
- Baking preserves nutrients and creates a crispy texture.
- A low-calorie and nutrient-dense snack.

Ingredients

- 4 cups kale, washed and dried
- 1 tablespoon olive oil
- 1/2 teaspoon sea salt
- 1/2 teaspoon garlic powder

Mode of Preparation

- Preheat the oven to 350°F (175°C).
- Stems should be removed from kale and tear into bite-sized pieces.
- In a bowl, toss kale with olive oil, sea salt, and garlic powder.

- Spread evenly on a baking sheet and bake for 10-15 minutes or until crispy.

Nutritional Information (Per Serving)

- **Calories:** Approx. 70
- **Protein:** Approx. 3g
- **Carbohydrates:** Approx. 7g
- **Fiber:** Approx. 2g
- **Total Fat:** Approx. 4g

Serving Size: 2 cups.

Preparation Time: 15 minutes.

12. Spiced Roasted Chickpea and Nut Mix

Health Benefits

- Chickpeas provide plant-based protein and fiber.
- Mixed nuts offer healthy fats and additional protein.
- A flavorful and satisfying snack.

Ingredients

- 1 can (15 oz) chickpeas, drained and rinsed
- 1/2 cup mixed nuts (almonds, walnuts, cashews)
- 1 tablespoon olive oil
- 1 teaspoon ground cumin
- 1/2 teaspoon smoked paprika
- 1/4 teaspoon cayenne pepper
- Salt to taste

Mode of Preparation

- Preheat the oven to 400°F (200°C).

- In a bowl, toss chickpeas and mixed nuts with olive oil, cumin, smoked paprika, cayenne pepper, and salt.

- Spread on a baking sheet and roast for 20-25 minutes or until golden brown.

Nutritional Information (Per Serving)

- **Calories:** Approx. 200

- **Protein:** Approx. 8g

- **Carbohydrates:** Approx. 18g

- **Fiber:** Approx. 5g

- **Total Fat:** Approx. 12g

Serving Size: 1/2 cup.

Preparation Time: 30 minutes.

13. Caprese Skewers with Balsamic Glaze

Health Benefits

- Fresh mozzarella provides protein and calcium.
- Cherry tomatoes offer vitamins and antioxidants.
- Balsamic glaze adds flavor without excessive calories.

Ingredients

- 1 cup fresh mozzarella balls
- 1 cup cherry tomatoes
- Fresh basil leaves
- Balsamic glaze for drizzling

Mode of Preparation

- Mozzarella balls, cherry tomatoes, and fresh basil leaves should be threaded onto small skewers.
- Arrange on a serving platter and drizzle with balsamic glaze.

Nutritional Information (Per Serving)

- **Calories:** Approx. 180
- **Protein:** Approx. 10g
- **Carbohydrates:** Approx. 7g
- **Fiber:** Approx. 1g
- **Total Fat:** Approx. 12g

Serving Size: 1 skewer.

Preparation Time: 10 minutes.

14. Sweet Potato and Black Bean Salsa
Health Benefits

- Sweet potatoes provide vitamins, fiber, and natural sweetness.
- Black beans offer protein and additional fiber.
- A colorful and nutrient-dense snack.

Ingredients

- 1 large sweet potato, diced and roasted
- Black beans, drained and rinsed of 1 can (15 oz)
- 1/2 red onion, finely chopped
- 1/2 cup cilantro, chopped
- Juice of 1 lime
- Salt and pepper to taste

Mode of Preparation

- In a bowl, combine roasted sweet potato, black beans, red onion, and cilantro.
- Squeeze lime juice over the mixture, season with salt and pepper, and mix well.

Nutritional Information (Per Serving)

- **Calories:** Approx. 220
- **Protein:** Approx. 8g
- **Carbohydrates:** Approx. 45g
- **Fiber:** Approx. 10g

- **Total Fat:** Approx. 1g

Serving Size: 1 cup.

Preparation Time: 25 minutes.

15. Cinnamon Apple Chips
Health Benefits

- Apples offer fiber and natural sweetness.
- Cinnamon adds flavor without additional calories.
- Baking preserves nutrients and creates a crunchy texture.

Ingredients

- 2 apples, thinly sliced
- 1 teaspoon ground cinnamon
- 1 tablespoon lemon juice

Mode of Preparation

- Preheat the oven to 200°F (95°C).
- In a bowl, toss apple slices with lemon juice and cinnamon until evenly coated.

- Slices should be placed on a baking sheet lined with parchment paper.
- Bake for 2-3 hours or until the apples are crispy, flipping halfway through.

Nutritional Information (Per Serving)

- **Calories:** Approx. 100
- **Protein:** Approx. 0.5g
- **Carbohydrates:** Approx. 27g
- **Fiber:** Approx. 4g
- **Total Fat:** Approx. 0.3g

Serving Size: 1 small bowl.

Preparation Time: 15 minutes (plus baking time).

16. Avocado and Tomato Bruschetta

Health Benefits

- Avocado provides healthy fats and creaminess.
- Tomatoes offer vitamins and antioxidants.
- Whole grain bread adds fiber for satiety.

Ingredients

- 1 ripe avocado, mashed
- 1 cup cherry tomatoes, diced
- 1/4 cup red onion, finely chopped
- 2 tablespoons fresh basil, chopped
- 1 tablespoon balsamic vinegar
- Salt and pepper to taste
- Whole grain baguette slices (toasted, if desired)

Mode of Preparation

- In a bowl, combine mashed avocado, diced tomatoes, red onion, basil, and balsamic vinegar.
- Season with salt and pepper.

- Spoon the mixture onto whole grain baguette slices.

Nutritional Information (Per Serving)

- **Calories:** Approx. 180
- **Protein:** Approx. 3g
- **Carbohydrates:** Approx. 18g
- **Fiber:** Approx. 7g
- **Total Fat:** Approx. 12g

Serving Size: 1 serving (about 3-4 bruschetta).

Preparation Time: 15 minutes.

CHAPTER 6

Desserts and treats

1. Chia Seed Pudding with Mixed Berries
Health Benefits

- Chia seeds gives omega-3 fatty acids and fiber
- Berries provide antioxidants and vitamins.
- Low-calorie and high-fiber dessert for weight management.

Ingredients

- 1/2 cup chia seeds
- 2 cups unsweetened almond milk
- 1 teaspoon vanilla extract
- 1 tablespoon maple syrup
- Mixed berries (strawberries, blueberries, raspberries) of 1 Cup

Mode of Preparation

- Chia seeds, almond milk, vanilla extract, and maple syrup should be mixed in a bow
- Let it sit in the refrigerator for at least 4 hours or overnight until a pudding consistency forms.
- Serve topped with mixed berries.

Nutritional Information (Per Serving)

- **Calories:** Approx. 200
- **Protein:** Approx. 6g
- **Carbohydrates:** Approx. 25g
- **Fiber:** Approx. 10g
- **Total Fat:** Approx. 9g

Serving Size: 1 bowl.

Preparation Time: 5 minutes.

Refrigeration Time: 4 hours.

2. Greek Yogurt Parfait with Nuts and Honey

Health Benefits

- Greek yogurt is probiotics and also high in protein.
- Nuts provide healthy fats and additional protein.
- Honey adds natural sweetness with antioxidants.

Ingredients

- 2 cups non-fat Greek yogurt
- 1/2 cup mixed nuts (almonds, walnuts, pistachios), chopped
- 2 tablespoons honey
- 1 teaspoon cinnamon

Mode of Preparation

- In serving glasses, layer Greek yogurt, mixed nuts, and drizzle honey.
- Repeat the layers until the glass is filled.
- Sprinkle cinnamon on top.

Nutritional Information (Per Serving)

- **Calories:** Approx. 250
- **Protein:** Approx. 20g
- **Carbohydrates:** Approx. 20g
- **Fiber:** Approx. 3g
- **Total Fat:** Approx. 12g

Serving Size:

- 1 glass.

Preparation Time:

- 5 minutes.

3. Baked Apples with Cinnamon and Oats

Health Benefits

- Apples provide fiber and vitamins.
- Oats add complex carbohydrates for sustained energy.
- Cinnamon offers antioxidants and natural sweetness.

Ingredients

- 2 apples, cored and halved
- 1/2 cup rolled oats
- 2 tablespoons maple syrup
- 1 teaspoon cinnamon
- 2 tablespoons chopped nuts (optional)

Mode of Preparation

- Preheat the oven to 375°F (190°C).
- Place apple halves in a baking dish.
- Mix rolled oats, maple syrup, and cinnamon. Fill each apple half with the mixture.
- It should be baked for 25-30 minutes or until apples are tender.
- Top with chopped nuts if desired.

Nutritional Information (Per Serving)

- **Calories:** Approx. 300
- **Protein:** Approx. 5g

- **Carbohydrates:** Approx. 60g
- **Fiber:** Approx. 8g
- **Total Fat:** Approx. 5g

Serving Size: 1 apple.

Cooking Time: 30 minutes.

Preparation Time: 10 minutes.

4. Dark Chocolate and Berry Smoothie Bowl
Health Benefits

- Berries provide antioxidants and vitamins.
- Dark chocolate contains flavonoids for heart health.
- Smoothie bowls offer hydration and fiber.

Ingredients

- Mixed berries (strawberries, blueberries, raspberries) of 2 cups
- 1 banana, frozen
- 1/2 avocado
- 2 tablespoons dark cocoa powder

- 1 cup unsweetened almond milk
- Toppings: Chia seeds, sliced almonds, fresh berries

Mode of Preparation

- Blend mixed berries, frozen banana, avocado, cocoa powder, and almond milk until smooth.
- Pour into bowls and add chia seeds, sliced almonds, and fresh berries on top.

Nutritional Information (Per Serving)

- **Calories:** Approx. 280
- **Protein:** Approx. 5g
- **Carbohydrates:** Approx. 40g
- **Fiber:** Approx. 12g
- **Total Fat:** Approx. 15g

Serving Size: 1 bowl.

Preparation Time: 5 minutes.

5. Frozen Banana and Peanut Butter Bites
Health Benefits

- Bananas offer potassium and natural sweetness.
- Peanut butter provides protein and healthy fats.
- A satisfying frozen treat with minimal ingredients.

Ingredients

- 2 bananas, peeled and sliced
- 4 tablespoons natural peanut butter
- Toppings: Unsweetened shredded coconut, dark chocolate chips

Mode of Preparation

- Spread peanut butter on banana slices, creating sandwich bites.
- Dip each banana bite into toppings like shredded coconut or dark chocolate chips.
- Place on a tray and freeze for at least 2 hours.

Nutritional Information (Per Serving)

- **Calories:** Approx. 220
- **Protein:** Approx. 5g
- **Carbohydrates:** Approx. 30g
- **Fiber:** Approx. 4g
- **Total Fat:** Approx. 10g

Serving Size: 1 serving is approximately 4 bites.

Freezing Time: 2 hours.

6. Coconut and Mango Chia Seed Popsicles

Health Benefits

- Chia seeds offer omega-3 fatty acids and fiber.
- Mango provides vitamins and natural sweetness.
- Coconut milk is good in healthy fats and also add creamy texture.

Ingredients

- 1/4 cup chia seeds
- 1 cup unsweetened coconut milk
- 1 ripe mango, diced
- 1 tablespoon honey or maple syrup

Mode of Preparation

- Mix chia seeds with coconut milk and let it sit for 30 minutes, stirring occasionally.
- In popsicle molds, layer chia mixture with diced mango.
- Honey or maple syrup should be drizzled between layers.

- Freeze for at least 4 hours.

Nutritional Information (Per Serving)

- **Calories:** Approx. 180
- **Protein:** Approx. 4g
- **Carbohydrates:** Approx. 30g
- **Fiber:** Approx. 8g
- **Total Fat:** Approx. 7g

Serving Size: 1 popsicle.

Freezing Time: 4 hours.

7. Protein-Packed Chocolate Avocado Mousse

Health Benefits

- Avocado provides healthy fats and a creamy texture.
- Cocoa powder adds antioxidants without added sugars.
- High-protein dessert suitable for weight loss.

Ingredients

- 1 ripe avocado
- 2 tablespoons unsweetened cocoa powder
- 1/4 cup Greek yogurt
- 2 tablespoons honey or maple syrup
- 1/2 teaspoon vanilla extract

Mode of Preparation

- Blend avocado, cocoa powder, Greek yogurt, honey or maple syrup, and vanilla extract until smooth.
- Refrigerate for at least 30 minutes before serving.

Nutritional Information (Per Serving)

- **Calories:** Approx. 250
- **Protein:** Approx. 7g
- **Carbohydrates:** Approx. 30g
- **Fiber:** Approx. 10g
- **Total Fat:** Approx. 15g

Serving Size: 1 bowl.

Refrigeration Time: 30 minutes.

8. Blueberry and Almond Yogurt Bark

Health Benefits

- Greek yogurt provides protein and probiotics.
- Blueberries offer antioxidants and vitamins.
- Almonds add a crunchy texture with healthy fats.

Ingredients

- 2 cups non-fat Greek yogurt
- 1 cup blueberries
- 1/4 cup almonds, chopped
- 2 tablespoons honey or maple syrup

Mode of Preparation

- Baking sheet should be lined with parchment paper.
- Greek yogurt should be spread evenly on the sheet.
- Sprinkle blueberries and chopped almonds on top.
- Drizzle honey or maple syrup.
- Freeze for 3-4 hours, then break into pieces.

Nutritional Information (Per Serving)

- **Calories:** Approx. 200
- **Protein:** Approx. 15g
- **Carbohydrates:** Approx. 25g
- **Fiber:** Approx. 3g
- **Total Fat:** Approx. 8g

Serving Size: 1 serving is approximately 1/4 of the bark.

Freezing Time: 4 hours.

9. Peach and Raspberry Sorbet

Health Benefits

- Peaches and raspberries provide vitamins and antioxidants.
- Sorbet is a low-calorie and refreshing dessert option.

Ingredient

- 2 cups frozen peaches
- 1 cup frozen raspberries
- 1/4 cup fresh orange juice

- 2 tablespoons honey or maple syrup

Mode of Preparation

- Blend frozen peaches, frozen raspberries, orange juice, and honey or maple syrup until smooth.
- It should be served immediately or freeze for a firmer texture.

Nutritional Information (Per Serving)

- **Calories:** Approx. 150
- **Protein:** Approx. 2g
- **Carbohydrates:** Approx. 35g
- **Fiber:** Approx. 8g
- **Total Fat:** Approx. 1g

Serving Size: 1 bowl.

Freezing Time: 2 hours.

10. Cinnamon Baked Pears with Yogurt

Health Benefits

- Pears provide fiber and vitamins.
- Cinnamon adds flavor without additional calories.
- Greek yogurt provides protein for satiety.

Ingredients

- 2 ripe pears, halved and cored
- 1 teaspoon cinnamon
- 2 tablespoons honey or maple syrup
- 1/2 cup non-fat Greek yogurt

Mode of Preparation

- Preheat the oven to 375°F (190°C).
- Pear halves should be placed in a baking dish.
- Sprinkle with cinnamon and drizzle honey or maple syrup.
- Bake for 25-30 minutes or until pears are tender.
- It should be served with a dollop of Greek yogurt.

Nutritional Information (Per Serving)

- **Calories:** Approx. 220
- **Protein:** Approx. 8g
- **Carbohydrates:** Approx. 45g
- **Fiber:** Approx. 8g
- **Total Fat:** Approx. 1g

Serving Size: 1 pear with yogurt.

Cooking Time: 30 minutes.

11. Strawberry and Basil Infused Watermelon Salad

Health Benefits

- Watermelon is low in calories.
- Strawberries provide antioxidants and vitamins.
- Basil adds a refreshing twist with potential anti-inflammatory benefits.

Ingredients

- 2 cups watermelon, cubed
- 1 cup strawberries, sliced

- Fresh basil leaves, torn
- 1 tablespoon balsamic glaze

Mode of Preparation

- In a bowl, combine watermelon and strawberries.
- Toss with torn basil leaves.
- Drizzle with balsamic glaze before serving.

Nutritional Information (Per Serving)

- **Calories:** Approx. 90
- **Protein:** Approx. 1g
- **Carbohydrates:** Approx. 22g
- **Fiber:** Approx. 2g
- **Total Fat:** Approx. 0.5g

Serving Size: 1 bowl.

Preparation Time: 10 minutes.

12. Pineapple and Mint Sorbet

Health Benefits

- Pineapple is rich in vitamin C and enzymes.
- Mint aids digestion and adds a refreshing flavor.
- Sorbet is a low-calorie and dairy-free option.

Ingredients

- 2 cups frozen pineapple chunks
- 1/4 cup fresh mint leaves
- 1/4 cup coconut water
- 1 tablespoon agave syrup or honey

Mode of Preparation

- Blend frozen pineapple, mint leaves, coconut water, and agave syrup until smooth.
- It should be freeze for at least 2 hours for a firmer texture.

Nutritional Information (Per Serving)

- **Calories:** Approx. 120

- **Protein:** Approx. 1g
- **Carbohydrates:** Approx. 30g
- **Fiber:** Approx. 3g
- **Total Fat:** Approx. 0.5g

Serving Size: 1 bowl.

Freezing Time: 2 hours.

13. Chocolate-Dipped Strawberries with Almonds

Health Benefits

- Strawberries provide antioxidants and vitamins.
- Dark chocolate offers flavonoids with a rich taste.
- Almonds add crunch and healthy fats.

Ingredients

- 1 cup strawberries, washed and dried
- 2 oz dark chocolate, melted
- 1/4 cup almonds, chopped

Mode of Preparation

- Each strawberry should be dipped into melted dark chocolate.
- Roll in chopped almonds and place on a parchment-lined tray.
- Refrigerate until the chocolate hardens.

Nutritional Information (Per Serving)

- **Calories:** Approx. 150
- **Protein:** Approx. 3g
- **Carbohydrates:** Approx. 20g
- **Fiber:** Approx. 4g
- **Total Fat:** Approx. 8g

Serving Size: 1 serving is approximately 4 strawberries.

Refrigeration Time: 1 hour.

14. Avocado and Lime Frozen Yogurt

Health Benefits

- Avocado provides healthy fats and creaminess.
- Lime adds a zesty flavor without added sugars.
- Greek yogurt offers protein and probiotics.

Ingredients

- 1 ripe avocado
- 1/2 cup plain Greek yogurt
- Juice of 2 limes
- 2 tablespoons honey or maple syrup

Mode of Preparation

- Blend avocado, Greek yogurt, lime juice, and honey or maple syrup until smooth.
- Freeze for at least 3 hours, stirring every hour for a creamy texture.

Nutritional Information (Per Serving)

- **Calories:** Approx. 230
- **Protein:** Approx. 6g

- **Carbohydrates:** Approx. 25g
- **Fiber:** Approx. 5g
- **Total Fat:** Approx. 15g

Serving Size: 1 bowl.

Freezing Time: 3 hours.

15. Cucumber and Mint Granita

Health Benefits

- Cucumbers are low in calories.
- Mint helps in digestion and adds a refreshing twist.
- Granita is a light and icy dessert.

Ingredients

- 2 cups cucumber, peeled and diced
- 1/4 cup fresh mint leaves
- 2 tablespoons agave syrup or honey
- 1/4 cup water

Mode of Preparation

- Blend cucumber, mint leaves, agave syrup or honey, and water until smooth.

- Pour into a shallow dish and freeze.
- Scrape with a fork every 30 minutes for 3-4 hours.

Nutritional Information (Per Serving)

- **Calories:** Approx. 80
- **Protein:** Approx. 1g
- **Carbohydrates:** Approx. 20g
- **Fiber:** Approx. 2g
- **Total Fat:** Approx. 0.5g

Serving Size: 1 bowl.

Freezing Time: 4 hours.

16. Mango and Coconut Chia Seed Pudding

Health Benefits

- Chia seeds offer omega-3 fatty acids and fiber.
- Mango provides vitamins and natural sweetness.
- Coconut milk is good in healthy fats and also add creamy texture.

Ingredients

- 1/2 cup chia seeds
- 1 1/2 cups unsweetened coconut milk
- 1 ripe mango, diced
- 2 tablespoons shredded coconut

Mode of Preparation

- Mix chia seeds with coconut milk and let it sit for 30 minutes, stirring occasionally.
- Layer chia mixture and diced mango in serving glasses.
- Sprinkle shredded coconut on top before serving.

Nutritional Information (Per Serving)

- **Calories:** Approx. 220
- **Protein:** Approx. 5g
- **Carbohydrates:** Approx. 30g
- **Fiber:** Approx. 12g
- **Total Fat:** Approx. 9g

Serving Size: 1 glass.

Preparation Time: 5 minutes.

17. Cinnamon Roasted Plums with Greek Yogurt

Health Benefits

- Plums provide vitamins and antioxidants.
- Cinnamon adds flavor without additional calories.
- Greek yogurt offers protein and probiotics.

Ingredients

- 4 plums, halved and pitted
- 1 teaspoon cinnamon

- 2 tablespoons honey or maple syrup
- 1/2 cup non-fat Greek yogurt

Mode of Preparation

- Preheat the oven to 375°F (190°C).
- Place plum halves in a baking dish.
- Sprinkle with cinnamon and drizzle honey or maple syrup.
- Bake for 20-25 minutes or until plums are tender.
- It should be served with a dollop of Greek yogurt.

Nutritional Information (Per Serving)

- **Calories:** Approx. 180
- **Protein:** Approx. 6g
- **Carbohydrates:** Approx. 40g
- **Fiber:** Approx. 5g
- **Total Fat:** Approx. 1g

Serving Size: 2 plums with yogurt.

Cooking Time: 25 minutes.

18. Apple and Almond Butter Sandwiches

Health Benefits

- Apples provide fiber and vitamins.
- Almond butter provides protein and healthy fats.
- A satisfying and portable snack.

Ingredients

- 2 apples, cored and sliced into rounds
- 4 tablespoons almond butter
- Toppings: Chia seeds, sliced almonds, raisins

Mode of Preparation

- Spread almond butter on apple slices.
- Sprinkle with chia seeds, sliced almonds, and raisins.
- Create sandwiches by pairing two apple slices.

Nutritional Information (Per Serving)

- **Calories:** Approx. 220
- **Protein:** Approx. 5g
- **Carbohydrates:** Approx. 25g
- **Fiber:** Approx. 8g
- **Total Fat:** Approx. 12g

Serving Size: 1 serving is approximately 4 apple sandwiches.

CHAPTER 7

Beverages

1. Green Smoothie

Health Benefits

- It contains vitamins and minerals from leafy greens.
- High fiber content aids digestion and promotes satiety.
- Hydrating and low-calorie.

Ingredients

- 2 cups spinach leaves
- 1 cup kale leaves, stems removed
- 1 banana
- 1/2 cucumber, peeled
- 1/2 lemon, juiced
- 1 cup unsweetened almond milk
- Ice cubes (optional)

Mode of Preparation

- Blend all ingredients until smooth.
- Add ice cubes if desired.

Nutritional Information (Per Serving)

- **Calories:** Approx. 70
- **Protein:** Approx. 2g
- **Carbohydrates:** Approx. 15g
- **Fiber:** Approx. 4g
- **Total Fat:** Approx. 2g

Serving Size: 1 large glass.

Preparation Time: 5 minutes.

2. Berry Yogurt Parfait

Health Benefits

- Berries provide antioxidants and fiber.
- Greek yogurt offers protein for muscle maintenance.
- Balanced and satisfying treat.

Ingredients

- Mixed berries (strawberries, blueberries, raspberries) of 2 cups
- 2 cups non-fat Greek yogurt
- 1/2 cup granola
- 1 tablespoon honey

Mode of Preparation

- In serving glasses, layer Greek yogurt, mixed berries, and granola.
- Drizzle honey on top.

Nutritional Information (Per Serving)

- **Calories:** Approx. 250

- **Protein:** Approx. 15g
- **Carbohydrates:** Approx. 45g
- **Fiber:** Approx. 8g
- **Total Fat:** Approx. 2g

Serving Size: 1 parfait.

Preparation Time: 10 minutes.

3. Iced Green Tea with Mint

Health Benefits

- Green tea provides antioxidants and may boost metabolism.
- Mint aids digestion and adds a refreshing flavor.
- Low-calorie and hydrating.

Ingredients

- 2 green tea bags
- 2 cups hot water
- 1 tablespoon fresh mint leaves, chopped
- 1 tablespoon honey (optional)

- Ice cubes

Mode of Preparation

- Green tea bags should be Steep in hot water for 3-5 minutes.
- Add fresh mint and honey, stir well.
- It should be served over ice.

Nutritional Information (Per Serving)

- **Calories:** Approx. 10
- **Protein:** Approx. 0g
- **Carbohydrates:** Approx. 3g
- **Fiber:** Approx. 0g
- **Total Fat:** Approx. 0g

Serving Size: 1 glass.

Preparation Time: 10 minutes.

4. Chia Seed Pudding

Health Benefits

- Chia seeds gives omega-3 fatty acids and fiber
- Coconut milk add a creamy texture with fewer calories.
- Satisfying and nutrient-dense treat.

Ingredients

- 1/2 cup chia seeds
- 2 cups unsweetened coconut milk
- 1 teaspoon vanilla extract
- 1 tablespoon maple syrup
- Fresh berries for topping

Mode of Preparation

- In a bowl, mix chia seeds, coconut milk, vanilla extract, and maple syrup.
- It should be Refrigerated for at least 2 hours or overnight, stirring occasionally.

- Serve topped with fresh berries.

Nutritional Information (Per Serving)

- **Calories:** Approx. 200
- **Protein:** Approx. 6g
- **Carbohydrates:** Approx. 20g
- **Fiber:** Approx. 15g
- **Total Fat:** Approx. 10g

Serving Size: 1 bowl.

Preparation Time: 5 minutes (plus refrigeration time).

5. Chocolate Avocado Mousse

Health Benefits

- Avocado provides healthy fats and creamy texture.
- Cacao is rich in antioxidants.
- Naturally sweetened with dates.

Ingredients

- 2 ripe avocados
- 1/4 cup cacao powder
- 1/4 cup almond milk
- 3-4 Medjool dates, pitted
- 1 teaspoon vanilla extract
- Pinch of salt

Mode of Preparation

- Blend all ingredients until smooth and creamy.
- It should be Refrigerated for at least 1 hour before serving.

Nutritional Information (Per Serving)

- **Calories:** Approx. 250
- **Protein:** Approx. 4g
- **Carbohydrates:** Approx. 30g
- **Fiber:** Approx. 10g

- **Total Fat:** Approx. 15g

Serving Size:

- 1 small bowl.

Preparation Time:

- 10 minutes (plus refrigeration time).

6. Fruit Infused Water
Health Benefits

- Hydrating and refreshing with natural flavors.
- Low-calorie alternative to sugary beverages.
- Provides essential vitamins from fruits.

Ingredients

- 2 cups cold water
- Mixed berries (strawberries, blueberries, raspberries) of 1/2 cup
- 1/2 lemon, sliced
- 1/2 cucumber, sliced
- Fresh mint leaves

Mode of Preparation

- Combine water, mixed berries, lemon slices, cucumber slices, and mint in a pitcher.
- Refrigerate for at least 2 hours to allow flavors to infuse.
- Serve over ice.

Nutritional Information (Per Serving)

- **Calories:** Approx. 5
- **Protein:** Approx. 0g
- **Carbohydrates:** Approx. 2g
- **Fiber:** Approx. 1g
- **Total Fat:** Approx. 0g

Serving Size: 1 glass.

Preparation Time: 5 minutes (plus infusing time).

7. Frozen Banana Bites

Health Benefits

- Natural sweetness from bananas.
- Provides potassium and fiber.

Ingredients

- 2 bananas, peeled and sliced
- 1/4 cup dark chocolate chips
- 1 tablespoon almond butter
- Use Chopped nuts or coconut flakes for topping

Mode of Preparation

- Dip banana slices in melted dark chocolate mixed with almond butter.
- Place on a parchment-lined tray, sprinkle with chopped nuts or coconut flakes.
- It should be Freeze for at least 2 hours before serving.

Nutritional Information (Per Serving)

- **Calories:** Approx. 150
- **Protein:** Approx. 2g
- **Carbohydrates:** Approx. 30g
- **Fiber:** Approx. 4g
- **Total Fat:** Approx. 6g

Serving Size:

1 serving (about 5-6 pieces).

Preparation Time: 15 minutes (plus freezing time).

8. Cucumber Mint Sorbet

Health Benefits

- Low-calorie and hydrating.
- Cucumber is rich in water content.
- Mint aids digestion and adds a refreshing taste.

Ingredients

- 2 cucumbers, peeled and diced
- 1/4 cup fresh mint leaves
- 2 tablespoons honey
- 1 tablespoon lemon juice

Mode of Preparation

- Blend cucumbers, mint, honey, and lemon juice until smooth.
- The mixture should be poured into a shallow dish and freeze.
- Scrape with a fork every 30 minutes for about 2 hours to create a sorbet-like texture.

Nutritional Information (Per Serving)

- **Calories:** Approx. 80
- **Protein:** Approx. 1g
- **Carbohydrates:** Approx. 20g
- **Fiber:** Approx. 2g

- **Total Fat:** Approx. 0g

Serving Size: 1 bowl.

Preparation Time: 10 minutes (plus freezing time).

9. Avocado and Berry Smoothie Bowl
Health Benefits

- Avocado provides healthy fats for satiety.
- Berries are rich in antioxidants and fiber.
- A satisfying and nutrient-dense breakfast or snack.

Ingredients

- 1 ripe avocado
- Mixed berries (strawberries, blueberries, raspberries) of 1 Cup
- 1 banana
- 1/2 cup Greek yogurt
- 1 tablespoon chia seeds
- 1 tablespoon honey (optional)
- Ice cubes

Mode of Preparation

- Blend avocado, mixed berries, banana, Greek yogurt, chia seeds, and honey until smooth.
- Pour into bowls and top with additional berries or toppings of choice.

Nutritional Information (Per Serving)

- **Calories:** Approx. 280
- **Protein:** Approx. 7g
- **Carbohydrates:** Approx. 30g
- **Fiber:** Approx. 10g
- **Total Fat:** Approx. 16g

Serving Size: 1 bowl.

Preparation Time: 5 minutes.

10. Almond Butter and Banana Smoothie

Health Benefits

- Almond butter provides healthy fats and protein.
- Banana offers natural sweetness and potassium.
- A quick and energy-boosting beverage.

Ingredients

- 2 bananas
- 2 tablespoons almond butter
- 1 cup unsweetened almond milk
- 1/2 cup plain Greek yogurt
- 1 teaspoon honey (optional)
- Ice cubes

Mode of Preparation

- Blend bananas, almond butter, almond milk, Greek yogurt, honey, and ice cubes until smooth.
- Pour into glasses and enjoy.

Nutritional Information (Per Serving)

- **Calories:** Approx. 250
- **Protein:** Approx. 8g
- **Carbohydrates:** Approx. 30g
- **Fiber:** Approx. 5g
- **Total Fat:** Approx. 12g

Serving Size: 1 glass.

Preparation Time: 5 minutes.

11. Mango Coconut Chia Pudding

Health Benefits

- Mango provides vitamins and natural sweetness.
- Coconut milk offers a creamy texture with healthy fats.
- Chia seeds gives omega-3 fatty acids and fiber

Ingredients

- 1 ripe mango, diced
- 1 cup unsweetened coconut milk
- 1/4 cup chia seeds
- 1 tablespoon honey (optional)
- Shredded coconut for topping

Mode of Preparation

- Blend half of the diced mango with coconut milk until smooth.
- In a bowl, mix chia seeds with the mango-coconut milk blend and honey.

- It should be Refrigerated for at least 2 hours or overnight.
- Serve topped with the remaining diced mango and shredded coconut.

Nutritional Information (Per Serving)

- **Calories:** Approx. 220
- **Protein:** Approx. 5g
- **Carbohydrates:** Approx. 30g
- **Fiber:** Approx. 8g
- **Total Fat:** Approx. 10g

Serving Size: 1 bowl.

Preparation Time: 10 minutes (plus refrigeration time).

12. Blueberry and Almond Overnight Oats

Health Benefits

- Blueberries are packed with antioxidants.
- Almonds provide healthy fats and protein.
- Overnight oats are a convenient and nutritious breakfast option.

Ingredients

- 1 cup rolled oats
- 1 cup unsweetened almond milk
- 1/2 cup fresh blueberries
- 2 tablespoons almond butter
- 1 tablespoon chia seeds
- 1 tablespoon maple syrup (optional)

Mode of Preparation

- In a jar, combine rolled oats, almond milk, blueberries, almond butter, chia seeds, and maple syrup.

- Stir well, cover, and refrigerate overnight.
- Give it a good stir before serving.

Nutritional Information (Per Serving)

- **Calories:** Approx. 300
- **Protein:** Approx. 9g
- **Carbohydrates:** Approx. 40g
- **Fiber:** Approx. 8g
- **Total Fat:** Approx. 12g

Serving Size: 1 jar.

Preparation Time: 5 minutes (plus refrigeration time).

13. Apple Cinnamon Protein Smoothie

Health Benefits

- Apples provide fiber and natural sweetness.
- Cinnamon may help regulate blood sugar levels.
- Protein-packed smoothie for sustained energy.

Ingredients

- 2 apples, cored and sliced
- 2 cups unsweetened almond milk
- 1 scoop vanilla protein powder
- 1 teaspoon ground cinnamon
- Ice cubes

Mode of Preparation

- Blend apples, almond milk, protein powder, and cinnamon until smooth.
- Ice cubes should be added and blend again until desired consistency is reached.
- Pour into glasses and enjoy.

Nutritional Information (Per Serving)

- **Calories:** Approx. 250
- **Protein:** Approx. 15g
- **Carbohydrates:** Approx. 30g
- **Fiber:** Approx. 8g
- **Total Fat:** Approx. 8g

Serving Size: 1 glass.

Preparation Time: 5 minutes.

14. Sweet Potato and Cinnamon Smoothie
Health Benefits

- Sweet potatoes provides vitamins, fiber, and complex carbohydrates.
- Cinnamon adds flavor without added calories.
- A filling and nutritious smoothie.

Ingredients

- 1 cup cooked and mashed sweet potatoes
- 2 cups unsweetened almond milk
- 1 banana
- 1 teaspoon ground cinnamon
- 1 tablespoon almond butter
- Ice cubes

Mode of Preparation

- Blend sweet potatoes, almond milk, banana, cinnamon, and almond butter until smooth.
- Ice cubes should be added and blend again until desired consistency is reached.
- Pour into glasses and enjoy.

Nutritional Information (Per Serving)

- **Calories:** Approx. 280
- **Protein:** Approx. 6g
- **Carbohydrates:** Approx. 40g

- **Fiber:** Approx. 8g
- **Total Fat:** Approx. 10g

Serving Size: 1 glass.

Preparation Time: 7 minutes.

15. Spinach and Pineapple Smoothie
Health Benefits

- Spinach provides iron and essential vitamins.
- Pineapple adds natural sweetness and vitamin C.
- A refreshing and nutrient-packed smoothie.

Ingredients

- 2 cups fresh spinach leaves
- 1 cup pineapple chunks
- 1 banana
- 1/2 cup plain Greek yogurt
- 1 tablespoon chia seeds
- 1 cup water

- Ice cubes

Mode of Preparation

- Blend spinach, pineapple, banana, Greek yogurt, chia seeds, and water until smooth.

- Ice cubes should be added and blend again until desired consistency is reached.

- Pour into glasses and enjoy.

Nutritional Information (Per Serving)

- **Calories:** Approx. 180

- **Protein:** Approx. 7g

- **Carbohydrates:** Approx. 30g

- **Fiber:** Approx. 8g

- **Total Fat:** Approx. 5g

Serving Size: 1 glass.

Preparation Time: 5 minutes.

16. Mediterranean Hummus Platter

Health Benefits

- Hummus provides plant-based protein.
- Vegetables provide vitamins, minerals, and fiber.

Ingredients

- 1 cup hummus
- Cherry tomatoes
- Cucumber slices
- Carrot sticks
- Kalamata olives
- Feta cheese (optional)
- Whole-grain pita wedges

Mode of Preparation

- Arrange hummus in the center of a platter.
- Surround with cherry tomatoes, cucumber slices, carrot sticks, olives, and feta cheese.
- Serve with whole-grain pita wedges.

Nutritional Information (Per Serving)

- **Calories:** Approx. 350
- **Protein:** Approx. 12g
- **Carbohydrates:** Approx. 30g
- **Fiber:** Approx. 10g
- **Total Fat:** Approx. 20g

Serving Size: 1 platter.

Preparation Time: 10 minutes.

17. Greek Yogurt and Berry Parfait
Health Benefits

- Greek yogurt provides protein and probiotics.
- Berries offer antioxidants and fiber.
- A delicious and nutrient-packed dessert or snack.

Ingredients

- 2 cups non-fat Greek yogurt
- Mixed berries (strawberries, blueberries, raspberries) of 1 Cup
- 1/2 cup granola
- 1 tablespoon honey (optional)

Mode of Preparation

- In serving glasses, layer Greek yogurt, mixed berries, and granola.
- Drizzle honey on top.
- Layers should be repeated and finish with a drizzle of honey.

Nutritional Information (Per Serving)

- **Calories:** Approx. 300
- **Protein:** Approx. 20g
- **Carbohydrates:** Approx. 40g
- **Fiber:** Approx. 5g

- **Total Fat:** Approx. 5g

Serving Size:

- 1 parfait.

Preparation Time:

- 10 minutes.

18. Caprese Salad Skewers
Health Benefits

- Tomatoes provide antioxidants and vitamin C.
- Mozzarella offers protein and calcium.
- Basil adds flavor and nutrients.

Ingredients

- Cherry tomatoes
- Fresh mozzarella balls
- Fresh basil leaves
- Balsamic glaze for drizzling

Mode of Preparation

- Cherry tomatoes, mozzarella balls, and basil leaves should be threaded onto skewers.
- Arrange on a serving plate and drizzle with balsamic glaze.

Nutritional Information (Per Serving)

- **Calories:** Approx. 250
- **Protein:** Approx. 15g
- **Carbohydrates:** Approx. 10g
- **Fiber:** Approx. 2g
- **Total Fat:** Approx. 18g

Serving Size: 1 plate.

Preparation Time: 10 minutes.

19. Quinoa Salad with Roasted Vegetables

Health Benefits

- Quinoa provides protein and essential amino acids.
- Roasted vegetables offer vitamins and minerals.
- A hearty and nutritious meal.

Ingredients

- 1 cup cooked quinoa
- Vegetables (bell peppers, zucchini, cherry tomatoes)
- Olive oil for roasting
- Fresh lemon juice
- Fresh herbs (parsley, mint)
- Salt and pepper to taste

Mode of Preparation

- Toss assorted vegetables with olive oil, salt, and pepper.
- Roast in the oven until tender.
- Mix roasted vegetables with cooked quinoa.

- Drizzle with fresh lemon juice and garnish with fresh herbs.

Nutritional Information (Per Serving)

- **Calories:** Approx. 300
- **Protein:** Approx. 8g
- **Carbohydrates:** Approx. 50g
- **Fiber:** Approx. 8g
- **Total Fat:** Approx. 10g

Serving Size: 1 bowl.

Preparation Time: 20 minutes.

CHAPTER 8

Conclusion

Embarking on a transforming path toward a better, more balanced existence through the lens of a 1300-calorie meal plan has been both powerful and illuminating. In this comprehensive guide, we've looked at the basics of the 1300-calorie diet, the science behind it, and practical tips for successful adoption.

The road does not end with calorie tracking; it is about adopting a sustainable lifestyle that values nutrient-dense foods, smart hydration, and mindful meal planning. Understanding the value of each calorie taken and selecting nutrient-dense solutions allows you to not only manage your weight but also fuel your body from within.

From understanding the fundamentals of calories and energy to providing precise meal planning, this book has provided you with the knowledge you need to go on a successful weight loss journey. It has emphasized the value of nutrient-dense diets, water, and sensible snacking. In addition, we've addressed frequent issues, avoided traps, and presented a choice of delicious and nutritionally balanced dishes designed to fit smoothly into your 1300-calorie meal plan.

Remember, this is more than just a diet; it's a comprehensive approach to wellness. It's all about making informed decisions, developing a positive relationship with food, and cultivating a healthy attitude. You'll experience hurdles along the way, but with the tactics presented in this guide, you'll be well-equipped to tackle them.

As you end this chapter and continue your journey, remember that transformation is a process, not an event. Celebrate tiny accomplishments, stay focused on your goals, and be kind to yourself. The 1300-calorie meal plan is more than just a means to an end; it is a step toward a sustainable and meaningful lifestyle.

May this guide serve as a companion, offering advice, inspiration, and practical tips as you negotiate the complexities of a better, happier self. Your journey is unique, and the decisions you make now will influence your future. Here's to a life full of vigor, balance, and the pleasure of relishing each nourishing moment.

Cheers to your health and fitness journey.

DAILY MEAL PLANNER

DAY/DATE: _____

BREAKFAST

LUNCH

DINNER

SNACKS

GROCERY LIST

NOTES

DAILY MEAL PLANNER

DAY/DATE: _____

BREAKFAST

LUNCH

DINNER

SNACKS

GROCERY LIST

NOTES

DAILY MEAL PLANNER

DAY/DATE: _____

BREAKFAST

GROCERY LIST

LUNCH

DINNER

SNACKS

NOTES

DAILY MEAL PLANNER

DAY/DATE: _____

BREAKFAST

LUNCH

DINNER

SNACKS

GROCERY LIST

NOTES

DAILY MEAL PLANNER

DAY/DATE: _____

BREAKFAST

LUNCH

DINNER

SNACKS

GROCERY LIST

NOTES

DAILY MEAL PLANNER

DAY/DATE: _____

BREAKFAST

LUNCH

DINNER

SNACKS

GROCERY LIST

NOTES

DAILY MEAL PLANNER

DAY/DATE: _____

BREAKFAST

GROCERY LIST

LUNCH

DINNER

SNACKS

NOTES

DAILY MEAL PLANNER

DAY/DATE: _____

BREAKFAST

GROCERY LIST

LUNCH

DINNER

SNACKS

NOTES

DAILY MEAL PLANNER

DAY/DATE: _____

BREAKFAST

LUNCH

DINNER

SNACKS

GROCERY LIST

NOTES

DAILY MEAL PLANNER

DAY/DATE: _____

BREAKFAST

LUNCH

DINNER

SNACKS

GROCERY LIST

NOTES

DAILY MEAL PLANNER

DAY/DATE: _____

BREAKFAST

LUNCH

DINNER

SNACKS

GROCERY LIST

NOTES

DAILY MEAL PLANNER

DAY/DATE: _____

BREAKFAST

LUNCH

DINNER

SNACKS

GROCERY LIST

NOTES

DAILY MEAL PLANNER

DAY/DATE: _____

BREAKFAST	GROCERY LIST

LUNCH

DINNER

SNACKS	NOTES

DAILY MEAL PLANNER

DAY/DATE: _____

BREAKFAST

LUNCH

DINNER

SNACKS

GROCERY LIST

NOTES

DAILY MEAL PLANNER

DAY/DATE: _____

BREAKFAST

LUNCH

DINNER

SNACKS

GROCERY LIST

NOTES

DAILY MEAL PLANNER

DAY/DATE: _____

BREAKFAST

LUNCH

DINNER

SNACKS

GROCERY LIST

NOTES

DAILY MEAL PLANNER

DAY/DATE: _____

BREAKFAST

LUNCH

DINNER

SNACKS

GROCERY LIST

NOTES

DAILY MEAL PLANNER

DAY/DATE: _____

BREAKFAST

LUNCH

DINNER

SNACKS

GROCERY LIST

NOTES

DAILY MEAL PLANNER

DAY/DATE: _____

BREAKFAST

GROCERY LIST

LUNCH

DINNER

SNACKS

NOTES

DAILY MEAL PLANNER

DAY/DATE: _____

BREAKFAST

LUNCH

DINNER

SNACKS

GROCERY LIST

NOTES

DAILY MEAL PLANNER

DAY/DATE: _____

BREAKFAST

LUNCH

DINNER

SNACKS

GROCERY LIST

NOTES

DAILY MEAL PLANNER

DAY/DATE: _____

BREAKFAST

LUNCH

DINNER

GROCERY LIST

SNACKS

NOTES

DAILY MEAL PLANNER

DAY/DATE: _____

BREAKFAST

LUNCH

DINNER

SNACKS

GROCERY LIST

NOTES

DAILY MEAL PLANNER

DAY/DATE: _____

BREAKFAST

GROCERY LIST

LUNCH

DINNER

SNACKS

NOTES

DAILY MEAL PLANNER

DAY/DATE: _____

BREAKFAST

LUNCH

DINNER

SNACKS

GROCERY LIST

NOTES

DAILY MEAL PLANNER

DAY/DATE: _____

BREAKFAST

LUNCH

DINNER

SNACKS

GROCERY LIST

NOTES

DAILY MEAL PLANNER

DAY/DATE: _____

BREAKFAST

LUNCH

DINNER

SNACKS

GROCERY LIST

NOTES

DAILY MEAL PLANNER

DAY/DATE: _____

BREAKFAST

LUNCH

DINNER

SNACKS

GROCERY LIST

NOTES

Printed in Great Britain
by Amazon